Leading Schools in Challenging Circumstances

ALSO AVAILABLE FROM BLOOMSBURY

Changing Urban Education, Simon Pratt-Adams,
Meg Maguire and Elizabeth Burn
*Leadership of Place: Stories from Schools in the US, UK
and South Africa*, Kathryn Riley
*School and System Leadership: Changing Roles for
Primary Headteachers*, Susan Robinson

Leading Schools in Challenging Circumstances

Strategies for success

PHILIP SMITH and LES BELL

B L O O M S B U R Y

LONDON · NEW DELHI · NEW YORK · SYDNEY

Bloomsbury Academic
An imprint of Bloomsbury Publishing Plc

50 Bedford Square
London
WC1B 3DP
UK

1385 Broadway
New York
NY 10018
USA

www.bloomsbury.com

Bloomsbury is a registered trade mark of Bloomsbury Publishing PLC

First published 2014

© Philip Smith and Les Bell, 2014

British Library Cataloguing-in-Publication Data
A catalogue record for this book is available from the British Library.

ISBN: HB: 978-1-4411-3956-6
PB: 978-1-4411-8405-4
ePub: 978-1-4411-4546-8
PDF: 978-1-4411-5682-2

Library of Congress Cataloging-in-Publication Data
A catalog record for this book is available from the Library of Congress.

Typeset by Integra Software Services Pvt. Ltd.
Printed and bound in India

Contents

List of tables

Acknowledgements

We would like to thank the staff and members of the wider communities of each of the five schools in this research for their help and support. In particular, we would like to thank the five headteachers and their deputies who gave so freely of their time to allow us to interview them at great length, to respond to our email questions and to provide other data that we requested.

Phil would like to thank his mother Patricia for her infinite patience. She has devoted her life to supporting him throughout his youth, and this shows no sign of ending as he approaches middle age. His greatest thanks go to his wife Sarah for her never-ending belief in him and to his two daughters, Alexandra and Jessica, for making him want to be more than he is.

Les would like to thank his wife Sue, his son Steven, his daughter Georgina and his grandchildren Daisie, Lottie and Poppy for helping him through difficult times. He would also like to thank the many friends and other family members who have provided practical help and moral support. Particular thanks are due to Mr Jennings, Dr Sanghera and the staff of the Queen Elizabeth Hospital Cancer Centre, especially the Room-11 Radiotherapy Team, for helping him cope with his own very challenging circumstances and, in so doing, ensuring that this book was actually finished.

We are both grateful to Rosie Pattinson and her colleagues at Bloomsbury Publishing for their help and advice and also for their forbearance as we missed deadlines for reasons of ill health.

This book would not have been completed at all without the excellent support of Penny Brown at Good Impressions Academic Editing (www.good-impressions.net), for which we are thankful.

1

Schools in Challenging Circumstances

A great deal of educational research is carried out every year. Some of it is published, a little is used, but the majority sits on library shelves and has little or no influence on the lives of schools, students, teachers and communities. This book documents an exception. It starts with the outline of a research study which was undertaken on headteacher leadership in four schools in challenging circumstances, and reports the findings of that study. Those findings were subsequently implemented, and this book analyses the positive effects of that implementation in a case study of a fifth school. As well as outlining the theoretical aspects of educational leadership, therefore, this book takes the theory firmly into the realms of the practical, and demonstrates not only how measures to enhance leadership in schools in challenging circumstances could be taken, but also how they have actually succeeded when implemented in a specific school which had already been placed in special measures.

The original research explored the leadership of heads in one local authority over a two-year period. The interviews with the heads and their deputies in the Coalborough area (the local authority and schools have all been given pseudonyms) set out to identify how the heads in four schools tried to improve both the objective measures of school performance in the form of examination results, and the more subjective evaluations based on perception within the schools and their wider communities. The data collected by these interviews were used to identify a series of strategies that might be deployed to facilitate school improvement. Subsequently, an opportunity arose for one of the deputies in the original study to implement these strategies when he was appointed to the headship of a failing school in challenging circumstances in another local authority, Willbridge.

Challenging circumstances: Background and measurement

The schools in this study are considered to be facing challenging circumstances because they serve areas with adverse economic conditions (DCSF, 2009). Coalborough local authority is situated in an urban, former mining area in the north of England and is ranked highly in all measured levels of deprivation. The areas have high levels of crime and unemployment and staff in schools within the authority note that there is lack of positive parental involvement. Coalborough's schools have attendance rates below national averages, and many have teaching posts that have proved impossible to fill and that are currently occupied by temporary staff. This leads to a lack of classroom consistency that has a negative effect on the behaviour of students and a demotivating effect on the permanent staff, both of which are considered to be significant factors for schools in challenging circumstances (DCSF, 2009) and are key priorities to be addressed by the leaders of such schools.

Coalborough has worse-than-average national rankings on indicators such as attendance rates, number of students with Special Educational Needs (SEN) and number of students registered for free school meals (FSM). It is identified as a deprived authority using all measures of deprivation. At the time of the original study, Coalborough was undergoing turbulent times, which, in many respects, are still ongoing. Social and economic deprivation resulting from pit closures, failing schools and radical shifts in national educational policy have all contributed to this unsettled environment. While many other authorities have embraced educational changes and utilized them to ensure they progress at an accelerating rate, the national league tables (BBC News, 2008) reveal that schools within this authority have made modest improvements and have often risen and fallen without any clear pattern, showing no evidence of consistent improvement. Local authority districts can be ranked with the Index of Multiple Deprivation, which uses six different measures to compare deprivation relative to other districts (Noble *et al.*, 2008):

> The Index of Deprivation 2004...identifies that 26% of [Coalborough's] Super Output Areas (SOAs) are in the worst 10% and over 40% are in the most deprived nationally. Five super output areas are in the worst 2% nationally. In the Education domain 37.5% of the [town's] SOAs are in the worst 10% nationally. Statements of deprivation analysis are provided to schools detailing the pupils' SOAs and the index of multiple deprivation data.
>
> (TEACHERNET, 2006)

Coalborough is ranked within the top 50 most deprived areas on each of the six district-level measures, ranging from position 19 (on the employment deprivation scale) to position 45 (on local concentration of deprivation, measuring the severity of multiple deprivation by focusing on hot spots of deprivation). The characteristics of high unemployment, low family income and households with education, skills or training deprivation create a community where aspirations are low and education is undervalued. Overall, the local authority is ranked as 41 out of 354 within England and Wales. It shares similar characteristics with many others listed within the top 50 most deprived areas, as grouped in the English Indices of Deprivation 2007 (Noble *et al.*, 2008).

Of the 17 secondary schools within Coalborough local authority, four have been placed in special measures by the Office for Standards in Education (Ofsted) within the last ten years, and three others were placed in a category issuing them with a notice to improve (Ofsted, 2006, 2007, 2008). One school left special measures and improved steadily for four years before dipping again and being placed back into special measures. This spurred the authority to take action, which it did by allying with a different authority where many of the schools are rated as outstanding by Ofsted. One of the schools within the high achieving authority was contracted to work with the failing school, which took part in the original research study. Within two terms under the new leadership, over 35 percent of staff had left or been removed, and six of the seven senior leaders were no longer employed. It was seen that change in leadership was the most important action required to enable the school to improve (Mercer *et al.*, 2010).

The developing policy and politics of schools in challenging circumstances

Removing headteachers and placing schools in special measures are, some would argue, relatively draconian measures (Bell and Stevenson, 2006). Partly as a consequence of such policies, schools, especially those in challenging circumstances, have been criticized and even vilified for perceived or alleged underperformance in a number of different ways over the last four decades. These criticisms have ranged from attacks on philosophy and pedagogy to claims about poor discipline and unacceptable pupil attainment. Such criticisms have emanated from sources including both politicians and the media. Much of this vilification, especially from the 1970s onwards, took the form of disguised attacks on the concepts of progressive and egalitarian education. Such attacks were fuelled by the Black Papers on education over a period of eight years from 1969 (Cox and Boyson, 1975, 1977; Cox and Dyson, 1969a, 1969b, 1970).

All the Black Papers attacked progressive teaching methods, comprehensive education and the lack of discipline in schools. The later versions argued for school vouchers, parental choice and increased accountability, so that schools that could not attract students should be closed. The views of the Black Paper proponents and their supporters were given credence by the work of Bennett (1976), whose study of teaching styles and pupil progress was represented as demonstrating that progressive methods did not work, although the study was widely criticized for its over-simplification of teaching methods and measures of pupil performance.

This academic argument became an actual power struggle in one primary school in Islington. The William Tyndale School affair put both political and educational ideologies on trial in a very public way when the headteacher introduced radical progressive teaching methods that were opposed by some members of staff. As Riley (1998) argued, William Tyndale School was, to some people, a school in which dedicated left wing teachers, who were trying to provide real choices and broad educational experiences for working class children, were vilified for their efforts. For others, William Tyndale was a failing school in which left wing-motivated teachers put ideology before classroom practice and created a climate of underachievement. Ultimately there was a public inquiry into the organization, teaching and management in the school (Auld, 1976) that apportioned blame to all parties concerned.

Power struggles over pedagogy, curriculum, autonomy and accountability continued within the education system in England and Wales over the next decade, through programmes like the Technical and Vocational Educational Initiative and developments such as grant-maintained schools. By 1985, a radical group of Conservative MPs was calling for education to be opened up to competition and market forces, although the rapid momentum towards what came to be called 'educational reform' did not gather force until the late 1980s (Glatter, 2012). The Education Reform Act (1988) not only introduced a prescriptive national curriculum, it paved the way for competition between schools through the publication of league tables based on schools' examination results and brought in a much more rigorous inspection regime which could, and did, lead to school closures.

Almost inevitably, those schools most under threat from closure by the new Ofsted were schools in challenging circumstances. One of the first schools to suffer closure was Hackney Downs Comprehensive School located in the Labour-controlled Borough of Hackney, the poorest borough in London. The school had a troubled history throughout the late 1980s and into the 1990s, and was used to teach pupils who had been excluded or who were truanting from other schools. In 1994 an Ofsted inspection reported that the school should be placed in special measures (Tomlinson, 1998). An action plan was drawn up to refurbish the school and provide educational facilities, but the required help was not forthcoming and in 1994 its Year 7 intake was frozen, causing a drop in pupil numbers. By this time some 60 percent of pupils in the school had SEN, the school had its fourth headteacher in five years and, in spite of the creation of an Education Association to run the school, the Hackney Education Committee ratified the closure of the school. Hackney Downs closed in December 1995 'with precipitate haste' (Tomlinson, 1998: 166). This was a classic case of a school in challenging circumstances, and the decision remains controversial to this day. Those opposed to the closure pointed out that Hackney Downs was singled out for special treatment by government to reinforce the government intention to close so-called failing schools. It is argued that academic results at Hackney Downs were not significantly worse than those at many other inner-city comprehensives, especially considering the problems it had inherited, including the nature of its pupil intake. Today, the site which was once Hackney Downs Comprehensive School is occupied by Mossbourne Community Academy.

The story of Hackney Downs is not uncommon. Many schools have closed since the inception of Ofsted inspections, but few have closed in such politically motivated circumstances, although recently many have reopened as academies following the Academies Act (2010). Established by the New Labour Secretary of State for Education in 2000 (Gorard, 2011), academies are schools in England that are directly funded by central government (specifically, the Department for Education) and independent of direct control by local government, although the latter is responsible for the funding formulae used to allocate funds between sections of education within an authority. An academy may receive additional support from personal or corporate sponsors, either financially or in kind; it must meet the National Curriculum core subject requirements and is subject to inspection by Ofsted. Academies are self-governing, and most are constituted as registered charities or operated by other educational charities. Most are secondary schools, for pupils aged 11–16. The Academies Programme has as its main purpose to break the cycle of underachievement in areas of social and economic deprivation (DFE, 2010). There is considerable doubt as to whether this has been achieved, and the Programme remains controversial, not least because it is argued that:

> the Academies Programme is an example of a neoliberal project because it is based on private interests marginalizing the public domain...what is presented as 'new', 'modern' and 'radical' is effectively highly conservative.
>
> (GUNTER, 2011: 217)

None of the four schools which took part in the original research project were academies. The school in which the resulting strategies were implemented, however, and which is the subject of the case study in Chapter 6, became an academy after its latest Ofsted inspection. It will be argued, though, that the school's academy status had nothing to do with its drastic improvement. The improvements were a product of the leadership strategies adopted by the new headteacher and the staff, who were largely already in post. It can be seen, therefore, that the history of schools in challenging circumstances and the education policies designed to improve pupil attainment are testament to the complex nature of leadership in schools.

The role of leadership in challenging circumstances

Within this volume we use the results of both the original four-school research project and the subsequent case study to argue that the implementation of the actions outlined makes it possible to improve underperforming schools, which will obviate the necessity to close them or to make drastic staff changes. This argument is based on an examination of the perceptions of their own leadership styles, which were expressed by the headteachers of secondary schools in challenging circumstances. The ability to lead an educational establishment through political and socioeconomic changes, especially in an area of social deprivation, requires the skill to motivate, adapt and shape the attitudes of staff, students and the wider community. The changing nature of schools, the political context of the authorities within which schools are situated and the impact that poor headship can have on a school and its community all reveal the importance of good leadership in today's schools (Day, 2009). Jacobson *et al.* (2009) note that if schools are to succeed they must be led in a way that enables them to change quickly and develop more people, in order to build a greater capacity for achievement. This then ensures that the school follows a cycle of continual improvement at all levels, rather than just the criteria currently being used to judge schools; if this does not happen, the school may subsequently be found lacking as these criteria change.

There are many different approaches to leadership, some of which overlap and interchange depending on the task in hand. Leadership styles and traits are complex and intricate entities that evolve over time depending on the desired outcomes, the people available to achieve these and the expectations of the leaders themselves. The analysis here derives its conceptual framework from existing work on transactional and transformational leadership since, as Eagly *et al.* (2003) and Bass and Riggio (2006) have noted, transformational leadership is an extremely successful method of improving school performance. As Leithwood *et al.* (2011) maintain, however, leadership in schools is about the exercise of influence, and the effects of such influence on student performance are mostly indirect. It is thought that a transformational approach to leadership may be the solution to these issues, as it involves all workers in the school's development and embeds a widespread enthusiasm for this development (Bottery, 2004).

Fundamental to the original research study was the now widely accepted view that it is headteachers who are mainly responsible for the generation of improvements within a school (Day, 2009; Drago-Severson, 2002). This is because, according to Liebman *et al.* (2005), headteachers are the major contributing influence on the school environment and shape the direction and ethos of the school by their behaviours. Weinberger (2004) draws attention to the long-running craving for good leaders in all walks of life, and illustrates the many ways in which a leader can influence both groups of people and entire organizations. This is even the case within a policy context where headteachers have not themselves been directly involved in the creation of a policy; they still act as the interface between the policy and the organization, interpreting external policy requirements and applying their personal values and experience to these policies to shape them in a particular manner (Bell and Stevenson, 2006).

When the range of possible changes that a headteacher can make is taken into account, it becomes apparent that the headship role is crucial for the success of a school. The benefits a school can receive when a headteacher is focused on supporting adult development are described by Drago-Severson (2002), who illustrates the difference that this can make to the daily learning of children within the school. One of the basic assumptions of the original research study, therefore, was that the most direct route to school improvement is through the role of the headteacher. In order to explore this further, transactional and transformational leadership were chosen as the two leadership theories that have the greatest influence on headteachers' leadership styles: transactional leadership is very task-oriented and much less complex than the person-centred, inspirational leadership associated with transformational leaders (Drago-Severson, 2002). For leadership to be transformational, it has to focus on the development of individuals, empowering them to achieve more, become flexible and develop a strong belief in their own abilities.

Although leadership is often considered to be a personal journey (Bowen, 1995), it is hoped that this book will, in some way, illuminate this journey for others and show how the influences to which Leithwood *et al.* (2011) refer might be exerted. It may enable new headteachers to accelerate their development, avoid pitfalls and build on the experience of others to move the schools forward, whilst also providing a clearer path to personal achievement and school improvement for more experienced headteachers. As Jorgenson (2006) noted, although learning how to be a successful headteacher was a fulfilling journey, it would have been helpful to be provided with signposts from others who had already travelled this road.

Many others have undertaken research into the effective leadership of schools in challenging circumstances (Brighouse, 2004; Day, 2004; Harris, 2002, for example). As Day, in particular, argues:

It requires passion to maintain a commitment over time, courage to persist in caring for every student in the class, those who are able, those who are not, those who are interested and those who are alienated. It takes passion to continue to believe in and be actively engaged in one's moral purposes and not to default under pressures of effort and energy.

(DAY, 2004: 436)

In the two studies reported here, however, the ways in which such passion can lead to school improvement are explored through transactional and transformational leadership. These are used to examine the detail of what the headteachers do and to explore the reasons behind the leadership choices they make. The studies also go further by exploring how such choices are related to the values that headteachers hold, and how these values are translated into action.

The complex nature of leadership has provided a platform for many researchers to explore and attempt to classify what is deemed as successful or unsuccessful leadership. This provided the starting point for the first research study outlined in this volume. The rationale was to identify where and when headteachers adopted particular approaches to leadership, and the benefits of these approaches. It was argued that the identification of headteachers' preferred styles, when coupled with the reasons associated with the decisions for favouring these styles, resulted in greater understanding of the successful leadership of schools, especially those in challenging circumstances.

Thus, this study addressed the significance of transactional and transformational leadership to schools in challenging circumstances and provided an analysis of the importance of leadership style to the particular socioeconomic circumstances associated with these schools. The extent to which headteachers regarded themselves as transformational leaders was explored by identifying which behaviours they exhibited that could be classified as transformational in nature. Such behaviours included vision and communication; valuing and building relations; handling unpredictability; using motivation to further achievement; and communicating their own values. These indicators of transactional and transformational leadership are considered through the perspective of the challenging circumstances experienced by the schools and communities in this study, in order to focus on the importance of transformational leadership in this very specific context. The analysis arising from the first research study was then translated into action through a follow-up case study, in which the strategies identified in the analysis of transactional and transformational leadership were applied in a separate school in very similar challenging circumstances.

The schools in the study

There are 17 secondary schools in Coalborough local authority, the headteachers of all of which were invited to take part in a research study focused on the leadership of schools. Of the 17 headteachers, one was on long-term sick leave, four volunteered to be involved and a further head agreed to pilot the interview schedule. In all, therefore, almost a third of the available heads of secondary schools in Coalborough were involved in the original research study. Each headteacher was asked to nominate a deputy headteacher with whom they worked very closely, who might be able to provide a greater insight into the school's leadership. The study was, therefore, based on an opportunity sample of schools. While this has the benefits of a possible increase in openness and a collegial approach to answering questions candidly, there was a danger that it might not be a true representation of the available population. Perhaps one of the major weaknesses in any small sample is that it is unlikely to represent a true picture of all schools. A comparison of the headteachers in the sample with the heads of other schools in Coalborough, however, seemed to indicate that the sample was typical of the secondary heads in this authority. Ultimately, this assessment was borne out by the extent to which the strategies identified were successfully transferred to another school setting. As Lincoln and Guba (1985) note:

> the degree of transferability is a direct function of the similarity between the two contexts, what we shall call 'fittingness'. Fittingness is defined as the degree of congruence between sending and receiving contexts. If Context A and Context B are 'sufficiently' congruent, then working hypotheses from the sending originating context may be applicable in the receiving context.
>
> (LINCOLN AND GUBA, 1985: 124)

The schools in this sample were not only similar to others in the local authority, but also to many schools elsewhere in the country, especially in examining areas where there are still considered to be extremely high levels of deprivation (Noble et al., 2008).

The four schools in the first research study were each given a fictitious name (Blackwood, Raleigh, Greville and Yarborough) to protect their identities. Each individual school has varying proportions of more affluent and poorer areas from which it draws its pupils. Raleigh School is in a relatively more affluent area than the other three schools. Its attendance rate is slightly higher than the national average, while its SEN and FSM rates are slightly worse than the national average. Nevertheless, Raleigh School is located within Coalborough, a poorly ranked local authority, and it draws a significant proportion of its pupils from areas with serious social problems. The other three schools are all below national averages on attendance rates and SEN. Although they have differing proportions, Coalborough on the whole is deprived, and as such each of the four schools shares characteristics related to this. Brighouse (2004) noted this phenomenon when he described how schools in predominantly white ex-mining towns share issues arising from high levels of long-term unemployment. These characteristics include high turnover of staff, difficulties recruiting staff, concerns with student behaviour, and the number of families who are switched off from education and find it hard to see how education can make a difference to their lives. This means that many students are typically not seen as self-starters with good personal learning skills. Instead they rely heavily on the input of the teacher. As Brighouse (2004) notes, a committed, caring teacher can make these students excel in even the most unexpected of subjects.

The students at three of the schools, Blackwood, Greville and Yarborough, fall within the 11–18 years age range, whilst those at Raleigh School have an age range of 11–16 years. All four schools are designated as secondary community schools. A community school is run by the local authority, which employs the staff, owns the school and controls the admission processes that allocate students to schools. In addition, community schools are expected to form strong links with the community they serve by sharing resources or offering community courses (DirectGov, 2010). When the measurements of levels of disadvantage and deprivation are considered, the students from Raleigh School are deemed to be broadly average (Ofsted, 2006, 2007, 2008). However, the students at Blackwood, Greville and Yarborough schools have been identified as significantly below average. Whereas at Raleigh School the achievement of students has been consistent, around 58–60 percent throughout the previous four years, achievement in the other three schools has shown variations, resulting in fluctuating results which have either risen above or fallen below the Government's benchmark score of 30 percent during the last four years. If schools fall below this benchmark, it may trigger an early inspection from Ofsted.

Three of the headteachers had been in post for at least five years, with the Blackwood School headteacher being the exception; she was appointed two terms before the study began and this was her first headship. Greville School is the smallest, having only 780 students, which places it as a smaller-than-average comprehensive school in the country, whereas the other three are all larger than average, each with over 1,100 students. As regards gender balance, Blackwood School has a female headteacher and male deputy headteacher.

Greville School and Raleigh School both have a male headteacher and female deputy headteacher, and Yarborough School has both a headteacher and a deputy who are male. At three of the schools, the interviews were carried out at the school itself; however, the headteacher and deputy of Greville School both requested that they be interviewed off-site.

These four schools, which formed the original research study, varied both in the number of students on roll and in their academic abilities and achievement. They were, however, situated in close proximity to each other and accessed similar student types from the same ex-mining community. The opportunity sample, while not representative through random sampling, is in many ways typical of schools in Coalborough local authority because of the spread in GCSE results, the catchment areas served, the student age ranges, the impact on value-added achievements and the similarly challenging circumstances faced.

The ranking position of the schools which took part in the study, compared with other schools within the authority, is shown in Table 1.1, which is a compilation of the standardized, moderated national results. This summary identifies the current measure of five GCSEs at grades A* to C including English and mathematics (Chartered Institute of Educational Assessors, 2009) and the Contextual Value Added Score, which compiles the students' improvement in grades from entering to leaving the school, where 1,000 is the national average.

This one-year snapshot at the start of the study provided a crude ranking system for the schools, but a better indication of their performance is to consider the progress they made in GCSE performance over a four-year period. Raleigh School had maintained a consistent performance since 2005, which is consistently higher than the Coalborough and national averages. The Ofsted Inspection Report for the school provides a description of the school's

TABLE 1.1 Statistical achievement of schools within Coalborough local authority (LA)

School name	Percentage of students achieving equivalent to five GCSEs at grades A* to C including English and Maths	Contextual Value Added Score from KS2 to KS4
Raleigh School	60% – 3rd highest in LA	1008.8 – 5th highest in LA
Blackwood School	35% – 9th highest in LA	981.3 – 13th highest in LA
Greville School	30% – 10th highest in LA	1010.7 – 3rd highest in LA
Yarborough School	28% – 13th highest in LA	981.5 – 12th highest in LA

Source: http://www.education.gov.uk (2008).

context and an overall grading used as a national benchmark for ranking schools; all of the inspections were undertaken within the last three years.

Raleigh School has 1,315 students in the age range 11–16. The headteacher had been in post for six years. Ofsted graded the overall effectiveness of this school as 'good' and provided the following description of the school's context:

> Pupils live in an area with broadly average social and economic indicators. A smaller than average proportion of pupils is eligible for a free school meal. A small number of pupils come from minority ethnic backgrounds. The proportion of pupils with identified learning needs and/or disabilities is broadly average. The school hosts a small local authority resource for visually and hearing impaired pupils. Specialist engineering school status was gained in September 2003.
>
> (OFSTED, 2006: 3)

Nevertheless, the area is one of significantly high unemployment and families in some parts of the catchment area suffer from severe deprivation.

Blackwood School's performance had improved since 2005, and was approaching the local authority and national averages. Blackwood School has 1,426 students. The headteacher had been in post for less than one year following an Ofsted grade of 'inadequate', which placed the school into special measures and led to the removal of the former headteacher. Since the appointment of the new head, two monitoring visits by Ofsted graded the school as making good overall progress. Ofsted provided the following description for the school's context:

> Almost all of the students at this above average size school are of White British heritage. The proportion of students with learning difficulties and/or disabilities is average. Students come from areas with higher than typical levels of disadvantage and the proportion known to be eligible for free school meals is above average. The school has specialist technology college status and has developed extended school provision.... The school has experienced staffing difficulties over the past few years. This includes the illness of the Headteacher. The Headteacher has recently been designated as the executive Headteacher and a deputy Headteacher has been designated as associate Headteacher with responsibility for running the school in the executive Headteacher's absence.
>
> (OFSTED, 2008: 3)

Greville School's performance ameliorated slightly after 2005, but did not show a year-on-year improvement. Greville School has 780 students. The headteacher had been in post for five years and was a deputy at the school prior to this. Ofsted graded the overall effectiveness of this school as 'good' and provided the following description for the school's context:

> [This] is a smaller than average school with 70 students in the sixth form. The school is in an ex-mining area...The area has an unemployment rate that is well above the national average and the proportion of students eligible for free school meals is also higher than average. The vast majority of students are White British. A higher than average proportion of students has a statement of special educational need and the proportion of students with learning difficulties and/or disabilities is average. [Greville School] has had specialist technology status since September 2003.
>
> (OFSTED, 2007: 3)

Yarborough School has 1,176 students in the age range 11–18 and is categorized as a secondary community school. The performance of Yarborough School had improved since 2005, but declined somewhat during 2008. The headteacher had been in post for ten years. Ofsted graded the overall effectiveness of this school as 'good' and provided the following description for the school's context:

> [This] is a large comprehensive school with the majority of its students coming from areas of high social deprivation. It has a higher than average proportion of students entitled to free school meals. There are lower than average numbers of students from minority ethnic backgrounds or with English as an additional language. The proportions of students with statements of special educational needs, or who need additional help with their learning, are broadly average.
>
> (OFSTED, 2007: 3)

None of the schools showed any high-level continual improvements and, of the four schools, three were below national and local averages in pupil attainment as measured by examination results.

These comparisons reveal that Raleigh School is consistently higher performing than the other three schools, with a Contextual Value Added Score above the average of 1,000. The other schools are broadly similar in performance; however, Greville School receives students of a lower entry level, and hence achieves a higher Contextual Value Added Score to match the GCSE performance of Blackwood and Yarborough Schools. The four schools are typical of those in the local authority, with two being above the national average for Contextual Value Added Score and two below. Interviews with the headteachers and deputy headteachers of each school explored, among other things, their leadership responsiveness to these levels of performance.

Two linked research studies on leading in challenging circumstances

The research study into headteacher leadership in schools in challenging circumstances was based on the assumption that transactional and transformational leadership can be identified by the decisions and actions taken by the headteacher. It is recognized, though, that these actions are influenced by what already exists, such as the resources available, the possible barriers to be overcome and the attitudes of teachers. A series of indicators were developed to establish the extent to which headteachers were transactional and/or transformational by examining the degree to which their actions were deemed to be transformational – person centred and inspirational, while also remaining vision-focused, fluid and flexible – or if they were reluctant to deviate from their predesigned plans and constantly focused more on the task than on the individuals achieving the tasks, as is the nature of transactional leaders. The comparison between actions which are deemed to be transactional and those identified as transformational was used to identify where transformational leadership was successfully deployed by headteachers in this research project.

The data collected were based on the self-reported perceptions of headteachers in relation to their own leadership styles, with more data being collected by interviews with one deputy head from each school to provide an additional perspective on leadership in that school. In research on educational leadership, there is a long tradition of examining the leadership and management styles of headteachers through self-reported studies. Ribbins and Marland (1994) show how the reflective perceptions of headteachers are linked very closely to the actions they undertake; this is corroborated by Southworth's (1995) finding that successful headteachers have high levels of self-awareness. Day and Schmidt (2007) state that leadership perceptions can be discovered using the testimonies of the leaders themselves, while Fairholm and Fairholm (2009) argue that using semi-structured interviews with leaders is the most appropriate method for collecting evidence in this type of study, especially if coupled, as in the current case, with other sources of data.

Data were collected for the study of leadership in challenging circumstances described in this volume using a qualitative methodology. The semi-structured interviews chosen started with predetermined questions, but allowed the scope of the interview to expand and the focus of the interview to change, depending on the responses given. Each interview was videoed, with the permission of the participants. The interview schedule was intended to provide an exploration of the extent to which transformational and transactional leadership were being successfully implemented within schools by the sample of headteachers. The questions were open ended, providing opportunities for headteachers to describe how they viewed their school, both in the past and in the future, with further questions identifying how headteachers handled circumstances that cause them to deviate from their vision; the responses could reveal if the headteacher is transactional or transformational in his or her approach. The questions also explored staff development and staff involvement, motivation, leadership style and personal values and motivations. The questions provided the opportunity for headteachers to reveal their commitment to developing individuals, their understanding of the school system as a whole and their links to the wider community.

A weakness in the interviewing process is that it is an attempt to understand the intentions of another. There are factors that make this difficult: the understanding of the terms and phrases chosen may have different implications for different individuals. In addition, the interview process requires the headteacher to report actions which may be filtered through their awareness of their intentions and desired outcomes. Due to this, it is feasible that the headteachers may believe they deploy their leadership in a particular manner, whereas others may feel it is deployed in a different manner. It was anticipated that interviewing another member of staff, a deputy head from each school, would provide a counterpoint to the data collected from the headteachers.

A systematic process of analysing data was used in this study to facilitate the identification of key aspects of the headteachers' leadership strategies. Two pieces of software were used to achieve this: *Express Scribe*, an audio manipulation software, served to aid the transcription process as it allowed the audio content of the interviews to be repeated or slowed down for ease of typing, while *Transana*, a digital image management software, enabled the transcribed text to be synchronized to a video and audio output transcript. This aligned texts with sections of video, so video clips of each line were tied together and analysed in conjunction with each other, enabling the transcripts to be placed in context when reviewing and analysing the data. The video interview also goes some way to help include the context of the interview by capturing the setting, the environment and the feel of the actual setting (Gillham, 2005). This is an important factor, since the environment in which the leadership is taking place is not separate either from the leader or indeed from the leadership actions. The video interviews provided an opportunity to analyse the data in more depth, identifying not only what was actually said by the headteacher, but also the way in which it was said. By watching the video again at a later date it is possible to revisit inferences from the interview that would otherwise have been lost by a written or even an audio account of the interview.

A step-by-step approach to coding interviews (Foster, 2006), using the transcription to create inductive categories and themes, was adopted for this study. Analysis software can speed up the linking and analysing of common themes and can also give instant analyses of key words or phrases.

MAXQDA2007 software was used because it allows full coding, cross-referencing and searching and also facilitates hierarchical coding and weighted scores to be assigned to texts.

Data for the second element of the research, which analysed the implementation of the strategies derived from the findings of the first study, were collected using a similar approach. A series of semi-structured interviews were carried out with the headteacher of Packwood School, the Willbridge academy now led by one of the former deputy headteachers from Coalborough. Data were also collected from an opportunity sample of members of staff and parents. The roles of people interviewed included: a head of mathematics, a second in science, a humanities teacher, a second in MFL, a Spanish teacher, two members of support staff and two parents. In addition, questionnaires were sent out to students, parents, staff and governors, responses being received from 19 members of teaching staff, 17 students, 2 governors and 7 parents. Details of Packwood School and the data collected will be presented in Chapter 6.

In summary, the research study of headteacher leadership of schools in challenging circumstances set out to identify those strategies deployed by a group of heads that proved to be successful in so far as pupil achievement in those schools improved over time and relationships within the school and with the wider community were strengthened. The study focused on the style of leadership provided by the headteachers and explored the factors that influenced them in deploying transactional and transformational leadership within their schools. It examined the extent to which these two approaches to leadership were deployed and how this was influenced by the challenging circumstances within which the schools are located. The detailed findings of this study are analysed in Chapters 3–5, while the case study of the implementation of these strategies is described in Chapter 6.

Transactional and transformational leadership provided the conceptual framework within which data were analysed and strategies identified, both in the original study of four schools and in the implementation case study carried out at Packwood School. In order to explore transactional and transformational leadership behaviour, key features of these leadership styles were identified through an analysis of a wide range of literature on leadership behaviour. This concentrated on what leadership is and what leaders do, in order to explore the complex distinctions between different styles and types of leadership. With this complexity in mind, the next chapter will examine the literature relating to leadership and in particular to school leadership. It focuses mainly upon four styles of leadership and different theories of leadership. Finally, it draws these together to conclude that the real distinction within leadership theories, both for empirical and for the analytical purposes related to this study, is between transactional and transformational leadership.

2

School Leadership: Concepts and Realities

In order fully to explore the nature of leadership as practised by the heads in this study, it is important to establish the broader nature of leadership and the attempts previously made by others to classify it. This will enable headteachers' leadership actions to be categorized in order to determine their nature and type. Several leadership theories are discussed in this chapter. This analysis reveals that leaders can – and do – adopt several styles, which are influenced by many factors. The political factors influencing educational changes are discussed, along with their implications for school leadership styles. There follows a focus on transactional and transformational leadership, and a consideration of the implications of these in the school context. The key features of transactional and transformational leadership are summarized in a way that allows them to be used to explore further the extent to which each approach to leadership was deployed by the headteachers in this study.

Concepts of leadership and management

Leadership is a contested concept. There are many views about what leadership is and one of the most common misconceptions appears to be confusion about the difference between the role of a manager and that of a leader. Vasu *et al.* (1998) separate these roles distinctly when they suggest that leadership is over and above the routines of management. They describe the processes involved in management and point out that a manager acts as an interpreter who negotiates with others to get the job done, while leadership is the process of attempting to influence the behaviours of others. Hiebert and Klatt (2001) consider leadership to be the process of moving a group or groups in a direction; their research findings highlighted that this should be in a non-coercive manner and will probably include some process of persuasion. The concept of a process of persuasion is supported in part by Murugan (2004), who suggests that while actions are taken by managers to achieve certain goals, those actions become leadership when they involve altering the attitudes and personal perceptions of others in order to influence their behaviours.

A similar view is taken by Marquis and Huston (2005), who state that a manager is one who accomplishes and conducts, whereas a leader is one who guides the course of action. Larson (2003) describes how leadership is crucial to the successful implementation of any major initiative. If this attribution of success is justified, then leadership is indeed the key factor when investigating the successful improvement of schools, especially when instigating change rather than maintaining current practices. The manner by which this is achieved, however, is open to debate and may, to some extent, depend on the leadership style being deployed.

Confused and contested leadership styles and theories

Accepting that, for the purpose of school improvement, leadership has a greater influence than management means that the analysis of leadership is paramount. Many styles of leadership lie between the two possible extremes of autocratic leadership and democratic leadership (Bush, 2011). Shell (2003) has identified other leadership styles, including *laissez-faire* and bureaucratic leadership. More complications arise when the substitute theory, trait theory, contingency theory or visionary styles of leadership are overlain on these classifications, and can be found to be either exclusive of particular styles or inclusive of many.

The main feature which appears to enable differentiation between leadership styles is the perceived leader input into the decision-making process. Furthermore, the advantages and disadvantages of each style may depend on the context in which it is implemented. Possible degrees of leader input are listed in Table 2.1.

According to Mero *et al.* (2000) autocratic leaders are indifferent to the needs or concerns of their subordinates and merely assign duties to them without discussion or negotiation. Shell (2003) discusses this style of leadership in terms of power, where autocratic leaders view themselves as the source of all power, as being able to make all decisions for an organization with absolute authority. The advantage of autocratic leadership is that all

TABLE 2.1 Perceived leader input into the decision-making process for different styles of leadership

Leadership style	Perceived leader input into the decision-making process
Autocratic	High
Participative/Democratic	Medium
Bureaucratic	Low
Laissez-faire	Very low/none

subordinates know exactly where they stand within the organization and know that their only concern is to carry out the instructions given by the autocratic leader. The main disadvantage is that all incidences of creativity are stifled, the skills and abilities of subordinates are often overlooked and the development of subordinates is largely ignored. Over time, such an approach to leadership will encourage either passive followership or alienation.

In contrast, within participative or democratic leadership subordinates play a major part in the decision-making process (Tannenbaum and Schmidt, 1973). Democratic leaders are very people-orientated and encourage employees to contribute to the decision-making process to such an extent that a bottom-up approach to decision making may develop instead of a top-down one, as created by autocratic styles (Mayer and Clemens, 1999). This is accomplished by encouraging strong lines of communication between employees and their supervisors. The underpinning reasons behind the actions are to treat employees with dignity and make them feel they have a valuable contribution to make (Mero et al., 2000). However, in practice many managers struggle to involve subordinates in the decision-making process to the extent required for successful participative leadership (Dorfman, 2004).

Extreme forms of participative leadership may be interpreted as a reluctance to play the leadership role or to abdicate leadership entirely. A different type of abdication occurs in bureaucratic leadership, which provides opportunities for leaders to distance themselves from the decisions and actions they may need to take. Bureaucratic leadership is almost a way for leaders to hide from the decision process, or at least to disassociate themselves from it (Owens, 1970). The bureaucratic leader follows the rulebook and must convince subordinates that the leader cannot deviate from it in order to help or take into account the views of others. Adams et al. (1980) refer to the bureaucratic leader as being more of a facilitator than a leader. They claim that bureaucratic leaders are not implementing their own styles of leadership but instead are implementing predetermined prevailing rules. There are advantages to this method in times when managers wish to remove themselves from a particular situation, or an unpopular decision (Shell, 2003). When bureaucratic leadership is exercised fully it should result in leaders acting identically throughout the entire organization. This may be viewed as advantageous, as it creates continuity and consistency across separate departments, but it could also be viewed as disadvantageous as it does not allow leaders to excel through individuality or to react to changing situations.

Bureaucratic leadership provides a method of advocating responsibility by hiding behind rules, whereas *laissez-faire* leadership is a method of abdicating responsibility by absenteeism or avoidance (Bass and Riggio, 2006). This is the most ineffective style of leadership and tends to be based on inaction. Within this absence of leadership, subordinates set their own goals and receive no support from their superiors. An obvious disadvantage is that everyone within an organization can be pulling in different directions, with no one encouraging employees to move the organization forward. There can be some advantages to this style of leadership if the team being managed is considered to be a group of motivated, capable professionals who are self-disciplined and have a desired outcome. In such cases this style of leadership will provide them with the freedom they require to deviate from existing paths and to develop new, creative methods and to respond effectively to rapidly changing situations.

It can be seen, therefore, that leadership is a complex and disputed concept (Hiebert and Klatt, 2001). Leadership style, however, is linked to the core values of the leaders themselves (Davies, 2007). An understanding of styles of leadership – how leaders do what they do – can only provide a limited set of insights into this complex concept. In addition to the different styles by which leaders exercise their power base, several leadership theories also need to be considered. Unlike leadership styles, leadership theories are not mutually exclusive, but some of the styles do provide a stronger leaning towards one particular theory than another. Table 2.2 identifies some of these theories and provides a brief overview of the key features associated with each.

Trait theory is one of the oldest theories of leadership. It is based on the Aristotelian philosophy that some people are born to lead. It argues that some people have particular characteristics or personal traits that make them more likely to be a successful leader than others. Drenth *et al.* (1998) show how the trait theory of leadership is based on the assumption that leaders have vision or charisma that their followers do not possess, but consider that it is impossible to find a single set of traits that guarantees good leadership. Furthermore, such traits are often abstract and difficult to define (Bush, 2011). Marquis and Huston (2005) conclude, after an analysis of a wide range of literature on leadership, that collaboration is more important than traits such as charisma.

TABLE 2.2 Description of leadership theories

Theory	What is it?
Trait theory	Leadership based on the personal characteristics of the leader
Contingency/situational theory	Leadership depending on events
Substitute theory	Leadership can be replaced by other factors
Transactional theory	Leadership as an exchange of rewards or punishments
Transformational theory	Leadership through motivation and increased self-awareness

Unlike trait theory, contingency or situational theory does not claim that one person has a range of characteristics that will guarantee success because here, it is argued, different situations call for different styles of leadership, and there is therefore no single preferable style of leadership (Boone and Kurtz, 2006). A good leader in one situation may not be a good leader in another situation due to one of the most important variables relating to the leader: his or her followers (Locke, 1999). Any leader needs followers, and it is impossible to examine the leadership without examining the group being led (Lambert, 2009). It is feasible that certain followers could result in a leader being successful irrespective of the leader themselves. This is a form of substitute theory and is an extension of situational theory, in that occasionally situations arise where variables are independent of leadership, and can substitute for the requirement of leadership. Clarke *et al.* (2006) provide examples of such variables and include ability, training and previous experience as factors that can lead to an effective performance from subordinates, even with unsatisfactory leadership.

Unlike situational theory, but building on the notion of contingent reward, transactional leadership is based on the idea that the leader plays a major role by directly affecting the behaviours of followers. This is achieved through transactions between the leader and the followers, since 'Transactional leadership occurs when the leader rewards or disciplines the follower, depending on the adequacy of the follower's performance' (Bass and Riggio, 2006: 517). Hence, both leaders and followers want something from the relationship and this exchange is the reason for their adopting the role of leader or follower (Marquis and Huston, 2005). Such transactions can follow two routes: one based on positive rewards for satisfactory progress and the other based on actions to eliminate failure to reach expected standards (Eagly *et al.*, 2003). Further, Bass and Riggio (2006) note that transactional leadership has two main factors: management-by-exception and contingent reward.

Management-by-exception can take two forms: active or passive. Active management-by-exception involves the manager taking steps to monitor quality and standards and then taking corrective action whenever work is found to be sub-standard. Passive management-by-exception occurs when managers wait for errors or mistakes to occur and then take action to rectify them. Both methods are reactive and are responsive to an identification of an unacceptable level of performance, which can lead to the demotivation of subordinates (Donovan, 1993). Contingent rewards, on the other hand, are based around subordinates reaching some agreed level of performance (Albritton, 1995). Contingent reward is reasonably effective in motivating subordinates to achieve higher levels of performance (Bass and Riggio, 2006). This is a process where the leader makes it clear as to what is expected and promises to provide some form of reward, such as a monetary bonus, if the assignment is completed to a satisfactory level. Bank *et al.* (2004) maintain that the future expectation of a reward can lead to a successful team performance and motivate staff. Management-by-exception, on the other hand, is used as a method of intervening whenever standards are not met (Bass and Riggio, 2006).

In transactional leadership, there is an emphasis on individuals' taking responsibility for their own actions and wanting to make a difference. This in turn increases the maturity of the subordinates and improves the conditions for substitute leadership and situational leadership, providing a more holistic leadership performance and an improved outcome. This basis of transactional leadership, where the leader–follower relationship is based on some form of transaction, does not always need to be monetary and can be the transaction of praise, or recognition (Hartog, 2003). If this is then coupled with a different perspective from the leader, such as the transaction of intellectual development, it can move towards transformational leadership.

Transactional leadership and transformational leadership are not two completely separate dimensions of leadership; rather they are end points on a leadership continuum (Hartog, 2003). Leithwood and Jantzi (2009) argue, however, that transactional leadership in the private sector is seen to fail in the face of recession. A similar process took place in education:

> The confluence of forces pressing on schools...resulted in a combination of heightened expectations for improved student performance, highly aggressive state and national policies for holding schools much more publically accountable and diminished financial resources. Schools were

being asked...to do more with less...There was just this minor problem of not having any sensible solutions, something analogous to passing legislation holding medical practitioners accountable for curing all cancer patients, even though no cure has been developed.

(LEITHWOOD AND JANTZI, 2009: 41–42)

From this situation emerged an appreciation that successful leadership is likely to be primarily transformational rather than transactional (Leithwood and Jantzi, 2009). Transformational leaders demonstrate qualities that generate respect and pride by communicating values, purpose and the importance of the organization's overall mission; they do this by focusing on the higher-order growth of individuals. As Bass and Riggio (2006) argue, transformational leaders focus on developing and raising the awareness of their followers about the importance of satisfying these higher-order growth needs.

The characteristics often demonstrated by transformational leaders include optimism, excitement about goals, a belief in a future vision, a commitment to develop and mentor followers and an intention to attend to the individual needs of these followers (Eagly *et al.*, 2003). These factors can be seen as instrumental in creating sustainable improvements within a school (Drysdale *et al.*, 2009). Consequently, it is possible to identify transformational leaders by their behaviours and by the response of their followers. Followers show a great deal of trust, respect and confidence in their leaders and identify with them as individuals, while the transformational leader is constantly nurturing optimism and enthusiasm throughout the organization, and will foster creativity and an environment where rethinking and the questioning of assumptions are in place. Most of all, every individual within the organization feels valued and involved, and believes that their contribution is important to the success of the organization, a result of the leader generating a very strong shared vision (Blanchard, 2010).

The notion of this shared vision is important to an understanding of transformational leadership because of its ability to motivate people to higher levels of effort and performance (Kurland *et al.*, 2010). Thus, vision is at the very core of leadership; it is the fuel that leaders run on (Hybels, 2002). Similarly, Kurke (2004) notes that leaders are in the creation business. Through the visualization of a different future, they change the world to be what they want it to be. The vision held by leaders not only serves as a map for future developments, but may be better understood, for the purposes of analysis, by locating any discussion of vision and values within the constructivist paradigm, which explores the links between values, vision and action.

The constructivist paradigm is a realization that what is believed to be true is entirely constructed within our own minds; a change of thoughts, therefore, can lead to a change of reality. Meaning is constructed and reconstructed based on new information, by overlaying our current beliefs to alter our future actions (Lambert, 2009). This explains how the external and the internal are linked through the constructivist paradigm in such a way that actions and the interpretation of actions cannot be separated from each other (Hermans and Dupont, 2002). Actions are taken to achieve an outcome, and this requires an understanding of both the outcome and the action; it follows, therefore, that understanding is specific to each individual's perception. The image people have of the world, and of themselves within this world, dictates the manner in which they will act, as 'The self needs to manifest his or her self through his or her actions' (Hermans and Dupont, 2002: 253).

Thompson (1995) explains how this perception of the world is considered by the individual to be knowledge, rather than interpretation, and informs future actions to such an extent that the knowledge becomes manifest. A perception that is believed to be factual knowledge can be so strong that it dictates every action, conversation and thought the individual has. When people hold beliefs that are this strong, the congruence between actions, conversations and thoughts moves them towards their perceived future, causing it to become manifested. The stronger the belief that people have, the greater this level of influence in manifesting their actions. For example, Gold *et al.* (2003) explored how ten outstanding leaders were able to embody educational values while still operating within the political arena. Gold *et al.*'s (2003) case study demonstrates that these outstanding school leaders were able to mediate policy through their own value systems, and were driven by personal values that enabled them to create a sense of institutional purpose and direction.

Policy contexts and realities

School leadership does not, however, take place in a vacuum. The options available to headteachers, the resources within schools, the organizational structures and, often, the immediate priorities are determined by broader educational policy made at a local or, more likely, at national level. Bush (2003) notes how pressures emanating from the wider educational environment and governmental prescriptions can leave headteachers with no room for interpretation and thus dictate the vision they must carry. Wright (2001) also claims that governmental involvement pushes leaders to act as managers and rewards them for implementing governmental changes ruthlessly. He terms this 'bastard leadership', and sees it as occurring when the values and direction of schooling are determined at the political level, and school leaders have to implement national programmes rather than develop policies based on their own distinctive values. The effect of this might be that headteachers are not always able to refocus external initiatives through their own value system and they may be deemed to be outstanding leaders only because they are very good at implementing governmental directions.

It is now no longer sufficient to just maintain a school. In order to meet the diverse range of needs of a diverse range of stakeholders, a school must be led (Leithwood *et al.*, 2004). Currently, the focus within schools is dictated by national educational policy; this informs institutional practice, including decisions about pedagogy and the content of the curriculum, staff performance and the development and allocation of resources (Bell and Stevenson, 2006). These policies are influenced by both global trends and local priorities. Lingard and Ozga (2007) illustrate how the political environment leads governments to identify actions they will or will not condone, which then lead to policy and in turn affect local authorities and individual schools. There are many examples of this that may be taken from the UK context. The *Every Child Matters* agenda, a framework for national change initiated in 2003, is a significant example. By combining the social and educational services available for children it was intended to change the nature and levels of accountability in order to improve the quality of services provided, so that every child could reach their potential irrespective of the personal obstacles they face (DfES, 2004a). This was to be achieved by providing national guidelines matching the duties of schools with those of other bodies to ensure they collaborate with each other and integrate the services offered for children and families. This required both that a level of conformity be established across organizations and that accountability should exist for each organization. Systems for monitoring and assessing the level of integration were needed to identify the successful, or unsuccessful, implementation of policies.

A similar emphasis on accountability can be found in the work of the Training and Development Agency (TDA), which holds teachers to account using a set of criteria within the professional standards for schools, against which teachers can be judged (TDA, 2009). These criteria provide descriptors of the skills, attributes and knowledge that teachers are expected to possess in order to be deemed as proficient in their role. Bell and Bolam (2010) note that such criteria then act as an accountability framework for managers within schools, allowing them to undertake a level of quality assurance across teachers and ensure a level of professionalism is in place. Armed with these measures of accountability, the government introduced a workforce reform that identified the duties that teachers can and cannot be asked to undertake. Blandford (2006) lists the changes that have been forced upon schools under the workforce reform initiative, including not only changes to the duties undertaken by teachers and support staff, but also to the broader leadership and management roles of concern to the headteacher, such as extending the school day to allow community access to enrichment activities, and the development and coordination of multi-agency provision for children.

She explores the change in the focus of current leadership practices to meet government policy guidelines. The implications are discussed by Bell and Bolam (2010), who describe the dilemma that arises for headteachers asked to balance long-term improvements with immediate results, and also their own vision for improvement with a set of external standards that need to be met.

However, Mercer *et al.* (2010) note that such reforms have made it even more difficult for headteachers to be autonomous or to lead through a reliance on their principles and ethics. Instead, headteachers are required to be accountable for continuous improvement in their schools. This, according to Ball (2006), feeds into incentives and performance-related pay, allowing poor-quality teachers to be penalized. Although the use of performance-related review is not limited to teachers, it is used in this case to ensure that everyone within a school is measured using criteria set by national policy, including headteachers. To ensure that these standards are met, the government provided funding for local authorities to employ external consultants as National Challenge Advisors, to work alongside secondary school leaders (DCSF, 2009). The government also assures accountability is enforced through the use of Ofsted, which has the power to sanction schools not meeting the inspection criteria (Mercer *et al.*, 2010). Government involvement, therefore, is intended to ensure that headteachers achieve the targets imposed, which forces them to become more task-orientated, concerned with national benchmarks of success and with statistical deadlines for achievement. As a result, heads seem to be increasingly pushed to move away from a leadership focused on the development of people towards a more reactive, task-driven transactional approach to leadership. Hence, the pressure to implement educational policies encourages headteachers to favour transactional rather than transformational activities. In reality, a system has been created where measures of accountability replace the freedom of contextual diversity, which then removes the headteachers' practices from their ethical base.

Thrupp and Willmott (2003) note, however, that although this level of centralization has taken place, effective headteachers can adopt and interpret the policies to align them with their own values in order to develop schools that have the skills and characteristics matching those considered by headteachers to be essential. This reveals how good leaders are able to adapt their practices to maintain their own internal values while leading through a changing political environment. Nevertheless, as Bush (2003), argues, while governments have the power to impose innovations upon schools, it requires commitment and enthusiasm to implement the changes effectively, and this is where vision, drive and influence of headteachers play an important role. It is this level of drive and vision that facilitates changes, both in existing practices and also in attitudes, beliefs and behaviours. The acceptance of this outlook reveals the importance of leadership within schools, where headteachers need to implement successful changes while working within policy guidelines.

Although tightly prescribed policies limit the extent to which many headteachers are able to facilitate the changes that they may wish to implement, Broadfoot *et al.* (2000) found that it was possible for national educational policy to be filtered through the headteachers' professional experience and then adapted to meet the realities of their schools. This process is explored by Bell and Stevenson (2006), who argue that when policy has been formed and a strategic direction for its implementation created, the policy is mapped onto the organizational principles to establish targets and success criteria. The implementation of the required changes is the responsibility of headteachers and such changes can then be mediated through the espoused values of those heads. Evans (2000) also argues that the actual leadership style is not as important as the extent to which values and beliefs are shared. She notes that it is not simply the observable aspects of headteacher behaviour that constitute this style, but also the hidden, internal values that lead to the headteacher acting in a particular way towards others. Headteachers who are dynamic and aware have much more of an impact than those who are set in their ways and have a narrow outlook on life, irrespective of the leadership style they implement (Evans, 2000). The process of fostering positive leader–staff interaction is much more important than the outward style of the headteacher, and headteachers get the best out of staff when they are able to motivate them by supporting and developing them as individuals. It is evident, therefore, that it is the impact that heads have on individuals and on the culture of their schools which generates successful leadership practices. This in turn can become a two-way process between leaders and followers, as leadership is increasingly devolved (Clarke, 2005; Poster *et al.*, 1999). The headteacher's behaviour patterns become mirrored by the leadership team and start to permeate all aspects of school life (Kay *et al.*, 2003). This is a feature of transformational leadership, where the headteacher is committed both morally and intellectually to the school and thus inspires others to new heights. Transformational leadership, therefore, is essentially value driven. It is the values that provide a sense of purpose and direction while enabling heads to be flexible in the approach to leadership.

Transactional and transformational leadership: A framework for analysis

It can be seen therefore that a focus on transactional and transformational leadership can provide a framework within which to analyse the approaches to leadership adopted by headteachers in this study. The changing demands on schools and the frequent policy shifts to which education appears to be subjected can result in leaders who are only able to lead through uncertainty (Cheng, 2001). Change requires leaders who are able to motivate and invoke followers to perform better and take more responsibility for their own actions, enabling their organizations to become more fluid and be able to adapt quickly when facing the changing environment. These are some of the features present in transformational leadership. According to Fairholm and Fairholm (2009) the most successful schools appear to be those where transformational leadership takes place and the headteachers are leading through the levels of uncertainty to create value. Through transformational leadership, heads and their staff can contribute to raising the aspirations, confidence and prosperity of schools and their communities (Earley and Weindling, 2004).

The transformational leader, therefore, has the potential to change the very culture of the organization and hence help shape and develop it as the requirements of the environment change (Bass and Riggio, 2006). This is not necessarily the case for transactional leadership, which does not easily accept deviation from the operating systems and procedures that already exist within the organization. The organization is seen by transactional leaders to be mechanistic in nature, rather than organic and evolving. Jacobs (2007) notes that schools are constantly in a state of crisis. Hence, transactional leaders find it difficult to adapt at a rate that matches the changes in accountability, expected standards and social movements. This means that organizations that are led by transactional leaders are less able to adapt to change and meet changes in demands from their internal or external environment.

The implication here is that transformational leadership is more closely matched to real-world requirements where things are constantly changing and systems are not fixed, understood, or able to be predicted (Donovan, 1993). Transformational leadership, therefore, is better suited to the requirements of schools which are trying to adapt to improve both teaching and learning, while at the same time trying to respond to new educational policies, as it has the potential to yield greater achievements within schools. As Hartog (2003) states, not only do transformational leaders have a greater impact on the performance and overall lives of subordinates than transactional leaders, but there is also a very strong culture of trust between leaders and followers. Consequently, followers of transformational leaders are keen to take on new challenges because they have full faith in the leader's reasons for promoting them (Smith, 2007). This helps the followers to become more responsible and more proficient in their duties, and also develop them as leaders and role models for others to emulate.

Implementing transformational leadership in a school setting

The improvement of student performance and achievement is a priority for all who work in education, but is undoubtedly the main priority of school leaders. Drago-Severson and Pinto (2003) argue that school leaders can achieve this improvement only by focusing on teachers and attempting to develop them. Their case study concludes that students perform better when teachers are encouraged to grow and learn, enabling them to develop new skills that equip them to adjust and overcome obstacles that may be identified as barriers to student learning. Liebman *et al.* (2005) identified methods by which teachers could effectively achieve these skills. The methods centred around the school developing a professional learning community, creating a structure that focused on the development of all. The achievement of such a structure calls for a purposeful and deliberate move towards this goal, and requires an input of direct leadership. Liebman *et al.* (2005) describe the extent of this move by depicting how leadership emphasizes the learning community:

> Findings indicated the principal has the ability to recognize leadership qualities in others, the school's mission/vision is connected to student learning, a leadership team supports and maintains the professional learning community, communication and collaboration are important to a professional learning community, coaching and mentoring assist in developing teachers and empowering others to take leadership roles, and the development of a learning organization promotes growth, learning, and empowerment opportunities for all.

> (LIEBMAN *ET AL.*, 2005: 2)

Liebman *et al.* (2005) touch upon many facets of leadership including vision, intent and collaboration. The means by which these should effectively be undertaken are also alluded to, with the use of terms such as 'coaching', 'empowering', and 'promoting growth'. It becomes apparent, therefore, that the role of headteacher is important in the development of this learning community and is the pivot upon which success balances. Values are central to this success.

The most significant factor for leaders in securing these values is positive moral leadership linked to the ability to motivate and inspire followers (Maldonado *et al.*, 2003) such that leaders can raise the consciousness of their followers by appealing to their values and helping to secure a focus on high values instead of base emotions, such as fear. This requires the ability to inspire others and raise their belief in themselves, an increase in moral values, and a nurturing of growth at all levels. These are key features of transformational leadership (Taylor Webb *et al.*, 2004). Transformational leadership enables leaders to focus on important factors, adapt more readily to shifts in requirements and encourage a sense of enjoyment in learning and achieving, reducing the stress felt by individuals at all levels within schools. What characteristics, therefore, might be identified to establish the extent to which transformational leadership is deployed in schools?

It has been argued that transformational leadership, with its emphasis on values, enables leaders to develop and inspire individuals. This approach can in turn create a greater capacity for meeting future, unexpected developments and for nurturing the skills that enable people to become more self-reliant and independent achievers (Taylor Webb *et al.*, 2004). However, to facilitate the analysis of leadership action it is first necessary to be able to identify where actions are transformational and where they are transactional. Aspects of transformational leadership can illustrate how leaders become responsible for their own actions, emotions and results, which enable them to create their own experiences (Anderson and Anderson, 2001). This is the real strength of transformational leadership. It does, however, have its limitations (Northouse, 2007). There are no clear distinguishing parameters to separate transactional from transformational styles. Leadership actions are best interpreted as being at points on a scale between the two approaches. However, methods of classifying actions as transactional or transformational can be identified, providing a means for the categorization of actions taken by headteachers.

Based on the analysis of transformational and transactional leadership outlined above, it is possible to summarize the key features of transactional and transformational leadership into a range of broad classifications. Transactional leadership is described by Albritton (1995) as leadership where the leader utilizes reward as a means of motivation, and expects some level of performance in return. This view is shared by Marquis and Huston (2005), who explain how both the follower and the leader want something from the relationship; the leader focuses on the task to be achieved, rather than on the person undertaking the task. The use of this task orientation creates a measure that can be used to judge standards, and, according to Bass and Riggio (2006), transactional leaders take steps to monitor quality and standards and then take reactive measures in response to the findings of these measures. Transactional leaders who use external measures to identify success are less likely to accept variations from these criteria. Bass and Riggio (2006) argue that transactional leaders do not easily accept deviation from the operating systems and procedures that already exist within the organization, and are reluctant to accept changes in these procedures.

The key features of transformational leaders, as identified by Eagly *et al.* (2003), are being optimistic and excited about a future vision. People feature prominently in this future vision and one of the main points of focus for transformational leaders is their intention to develop and mentor followers (Drysdale *et al.*, 2009). Transformational leaders are very person-centred and are constantly nurturing optimism and enthusiasm throughout the organization, empowering subordinates to do more than they ever expected they could do (Albritton, 1995). This is achieved by inspiring people, showing them that someone has a real belief in them as an individual and will provide continuous support to enable them to become more than they currently are. This level of inspiration is identified as the means by which transformational leaders address the followers' sense of self-worth and raise them to a level where they have a true commitment and involvement (Bass and Riggio, 2006).

It has been argued that transformational leaders, who stimulate and inspire followers to achieve extraordinary outcomes, also develop their own leadership capacity by linking their actions to their intrinsic core values and beliefs (Leithwood and Jantzi, 2009). Hartog (2003) argues that transformational leaders have high levels of integrity, while Harris (2003) finds that transformational leaders use their core values to develop high expectations and high values in others. Southworth (1998) describes how transformational leaders constantly question their own values and practices in order to question the paradigm in which their values are contained. This in turn results in leaders themselves being able to change, an integral part of being transformational. This view is shared by Denny (2001), who stresses the importance of good leaders becoming more self-aware, having a greater understanding of all aspects of themselves and developing their emotional intelligence. This ability to change themselves results in leaders who are fluid and flexible in their approach, constantly questioning and refining the thoughts behind their actions. A summary of the indicators by which transactional and transformational leadership can be identified in the work of headteachers in this study is listed in Table 2.3. These indicators were used to explore how far transactional and transformational leadership were deployed by the heads of four schools in challenging circumstances.

In conclusion, it has been argued that the leadership of headteachers is key to the success of any school. Headteacher leadership can best be understood in terms of transactional and transformational leadership, the key features of which have been identified. While it can be argued that transformational leadership might be the most effective method of leading a school due to the extent to which it can facilitate improvements in the achievements of students,

TABLE 2.3 Indicators of transactional and transformational leadership

Transactional leadership	Transformational leadership
Focused on task	Person-centred
Focuses on standards	Vision-focused
Uses external measures	Links to core values
Reactive and responsive	Developing and changing
Does not easily accept deviation	Fluid and flexible
Utilizes rewards as motivation	Inspirational
Does not change quickly	Able to change

provide personal development for all and prepare a school for success while in a unpredictable and changing environment, it is also necessary to consider the extent to which heads deploy transactional leadership and to identify the factors which result in the deployment of each approach to leadership.

3

Using Transactional Leadership in Schools

This is the first of three chapters outlining the results of a research study of headteacher leadership in four secondary schools in challenging circumstances. In the previous chapter, it was noted how Hartog (2003) argued that transactional and transformational leadership are separate dimensions of leadership. The data will therefore be presented from these two aspects in this and the following chapter, respectively, and the responses from each school will be categorized into examples of transactional and transformational leadership. These will be succeeded in Chapter 5 by an analysis of the implications of the findings and an examination of the evidence relating to the degree to which the success of headteachers and their schools could be attributed to transformational leadership.

It was argued in Chapter 2 that transactional leadership occurs when a transaction takes place between the leader and the followers; it becomes evident when the leader focuses on the seven indicators summarized in Table 2.3. These indicators are utilized throughout this research as the means by which responses from headteachers are classified as being either transactional or transformational in nature. One method of establishing the perceived importance of each indicator is to identify how often headteachers make reference to it throughout their interview. If a feature is considered by the headteacher to be of great importance it may be incorporated in several responses relating to different questions about the school. Using this data, the response categorizations can be presented in order of frequency: for example, the subsection with most recorded instances was that of headteachers being task-orientated, implying that this is seen as very important to them.

The outcome as priority: Focusing on task

Albritton (1995) showed how transactional leaders are much more task-orientated than person-orientated. Of the seven actions deemed to illustrate transactional leadership, shown in Table 2.3, the one most frequently cited by the heads in the main study was their focus on task. For example, the headteacher of Raleigh School, when asked about the formation of the school vision and the involvement of others in the creation of this vision, replied: 'To be brutally honest, at the start it was effectively just me.' When the head was first appointed to the role, therefore, he saw that the school needed a vision and that establishing this was more important than the involvement of staff and as such was not open to input from others.

Similarly, the headteacher of Blackwood School stated that she originally led the school using a vision that was: 'top-down, because of the very nature of the people coming in at senior leadership team level and saying this is how we are going to do things now'. Here again, in the headteacher's opinion, the task of establishing a vision for the school was best accomplished without an emphasis on staff involvement in the process. The deputy head of Yarborough School also noted this when explaining how the headteacher had set the vision for the school. During the interview he declared that 'It's been very much one leader in charge of a school, [who] does the total direction for that school and you get on board or you don't.' Again, this is an example of a headteacher centring on the task above all else, including the individuals in the organization, and is a strong indication of transactional leadership.

Another deputy revealed a similar example when he described the involvement with the headteacher of Blackwood School. The head of the school identified a number of areas that needed changing and the strategies for bringing about the required changes. The Senior Leadership Team then implemented those strategies. The Blackwood deputy explained that:

> first of all we had to put things and measures into place and it wasn't really open to consultation. It was about looking at a need, identifying where there was a problem and the strategies we could put in place.

The headteacher of Blackwood School also endorsed an emphasis on tasks when describing the training that had taken place. She stated how she had set the agenda for training by deciding what was to be delivered, and by whom. She commented that 'a lot of our development is whole College stuff which has to be done this way because it's about explaining [to the staff]'. The headteacher's actions illustrated her belief that training was instrumental in achieving these tasks and purpose.

A similar view was expressed by the headteacher of Raleigh School, when he described how the school evaluated the training given to staff. He stated that it was measured entirely by outputs. He approached the evaluation of training by asking, 'where's the evidence that it's actually being used, how effectively is it being used, what's getting better because of it and if nothing, why are we doing it?' This response exemplifies the headteacher's focus on the school-improvement tasks that he wanted in place and his view that training should be measured by the impact it had on his identified, measurable systems. The deputy of Yarborough School explained how they identify these measurable systems, using priorities that 'tick the Ofsted box' by creating a school improvement plan and tracking system that set a series of organizational goals that would lead to externally measurable outcomes. The method of achieving the goals in this plan was clarified by the headteacher of Yarborough, when he prioritized staff training into three levels and showed that his opinion of training staff is primarily about achieving the tasks associated with meeting the organization's needs: 'It is firstly about the needs of the organization, secondly it is about the needs of individuals and thirdly it is about developing skills and expertise.' This headteacher felt it was more important to achieve a desired outcome than to develop followers, a dilemma noted by Bell and Bolam (2010) as emerging when educational policy impacts on school leadership.

The headteacher of Greville School also believed that staff development is a means of task achievement. He reflected that:

staff development is linked to achieving that aim [identified in the school vision] by ensuring that the staff have got the prerequisite skills and knowledge to carry out their job effectively so that the department improvement plan – the college improvement plan which is based on the vision of raising aspiration and achievement – is in place and is running.

This again highlighted the transactional aspect of tasks associated with moving the school towards a predetermined goal by the pursuit of a series of identified, formalized tasks recorded in the development plan.

It was clear that in all the schools in the main study, staff development focused on the achievement of tasks. As the deputy from Yarborough School put it:

We have a formal evaluation like we would if you went on an outside course so they answer a questionnaire after what the purpose of it was, was it successful, what did they get from it, was the presenter up to standard.

In a similar vein, the deputy of Blackwood School noted how the Senior Leadership Team used the Performance Management cycle to check on the outputs achieved from training, which are 'evaluated through performance management'. In the Raleigh School, the deputy explained that their training was identified and evaluated through:

> the school development planning cycle because, wherever possible we try to keep things as coherent as we can in that people's developments should reflect [what is in the planning], it is not that we discourage free rein but if people are developing areas that are of interest to them they also ideally need to be of value to the school and by and large that's what's happening. They identify areas within their departmental development plan that they can take significant leadership of and the evaluation of that happens within the yearly cycle; performance management of course then plays a part because their performance management targets are related to this.

The transactional element of task orientation can be clearly seen as a theme running through these responses. Staff training was seen by school leaders as a means of achieving school targets, and it was evaluated by comparing it to a series of predefined tasks. This was true throughout all four schools, where the type and level of staff training were tied to the school goals and were evaluated, wherever possible, through measurable outcomes and the performance management cycle which was often linked to Ofsted inspection criteria. The limited nature of this approach, however, could create a level of central control that prevents teachers from exploring their own interpretation of professionalism. Instead they have external standards imposed upon them, which are used annually to measure their performance against a set of predetermined criteria which are linked to a school's evaluation of its own performance.

Many of the school leaders also tied the training to the provision of a level of sustainability within the school. This was illustrated by the head of Blackwood:

> It is about on-going structures; it is about sustainability of procedures and making sure that, and I keep going back and I'm saying structures a lot, that is quite deliberately because you cannot just have an idea and launch it and then just hope that it happens. There's got to then be genuine accountability.

Similarly, the senior management of Yarborough School had developed a formalized method of tracking and measuring on-going improvement outcomes, using a quality assurance folder they had developed. This held staff accountable for their outcomes and was informed by the Professional Standards for Teachers (TDA, 2009). The quality assurance folder consisted of a series of scripts and templates to be completed by all line managers to provide a systematic method of monitoring and measuring the tasks undertaken across every department within the school. Quality assurance folders were held – 'one for the line manager and one for the head of the department' – and provided a means of ensuring that departments remained on-task throughout the year.

The extent of the focus of Blackwood School's leaders upon tasks resulted in staff being issued with temporary contracts for these specific tasks; the deputy head explained:

> Contracts are temporary, so your evaluation really is, has this person made an impact, and it is measured then to see…here is your role, here are the targets that have been set for you through the year, and then have those targets been achieved, is this person right, do we renew this person's contract…not everybody is suited to leading an initiative and therefore, because we've put in twelve and twenty-four month contracts, it means that then we've got a timeline in which to meet our targets and that's what it's evaluated on…[following this evaluation we decide]…do we move this person forward or do we terminate the contract.

Student achievement was also perceived as a task-based activity, the purpose of which is to ensure as many students as possible achieve as many qualifications as possible. As the Blackwood School deputy asserted, 'it is about getting as many students to achieve as possible'. In this school students could continually re-take subjects or move between subjects when it becomes apparent that they will either fail a subject or become disengaged by it, a policy which illustrated the ethos of Blackwood School's headteacher that what was important in this school was that students should gain qualifications and that students should be actively encouraged to change subjects if they were in danger of not achieving a desirable grade.

As part of this overall approach, the education of students was seen as a task, the success of which was to be measured in terms of grades, rather than in the personal development of individuals. As the head stated:

> I am genuine in my vision, knowing that I come with a track record…of getting young people qualifications and once I've convinced people of that, which I hope I do on a daily basis, then some of the leadership is going to have to be a lot more tougher in terms of this is going to happen, and it's going to happen now, or next week, or by half term. It has to happen, and it's not negotiable and that's to do with accountability as well and people knowing that they must be fully accountable.

At Blackwood, this was not a people-centred process: 'I can rub people up the wrong way I think, but I don't mind doing that because I try and cling on to what I'm doing.' What was important here was the achievement of the task in hand, a feature of task orientation and transactional leadership.

The headteacher of Raleigh School expressed a similar view when he commented that:

> I reserve the right to say it will be like this because I do, and I will continue to, because at times . . . it is good to talk, but at times we need to do, and we always review, we do, we always review, but at times there's still . . . no lads, it's going to be like that, so just do it.

This headteacher, therefore, also took a task-orientated approach to ensuring his targets were implemented within the school, without question or consultation. Every headteacher in the study demonstrated aspects of this orientation towards achieving tasks, especially when first appointed. The cause may be the political context within which headteachers operate, which is clearly not unique to this study or to any one local authority, irrespective of the level of social deprivation. This emphasis on transactional leadership provides evidence that it may, at least in part, be taking place due to the political pressure to achieve results, meet targets placed upon schools and ensure they have evidence to provide to Ofsted that the school is continually improving. However, transactional leadership may be a feature of the attempts made by headteachers to improve schools in challenging circumstances when first appointed. Although there is no direct evidence that the headteachers in this study were transactional in their previous schools, analysis of the interviews did provide evidence that the headteachers had become less transactional over time.

Meeting the benchmark: The focus on standards

Transactional leaders often focus on the standards achieved by an organization (Bass and Riggio, 2006). In schools the concern with standards is closely linked to the focus on tasks since the tasks are often performance or attainment related. This focus on standards was the second most frequently recurring theme in the headteachers' responses. Throughout their interviews the heads and deputies of both Blackwood and Yarborough Schools often referred to their actions of holding people to high levels of accountability. The headteacher of Blackwood School stated, 'We have to have systems and structures where accountability is key and expressed a need for genuine accountability.' She argued that a system of continually reporting progress to a school leader was an effective method of ensuring accountability: 'the truth of it is that only when there's that type of accountability do we ultimately ensure that things keep happening'.

The headteacher of Yarborough School also recognized the importance of accountability and the framework established to ensure that teachers and heads are held accountable for what they do (TDA, 2009). He argued that being held accountable could be a tool both for empowering staff and for acknowledging that staff are performing well. Although the other headteachers did not refer directly to accountability to the same extent, it was still evident that they held teachers accountable for achieving high standards. For example, the deputy at Raleigh School commented that the headteacher expected her to 'maintain the quality of teaching and learning and performance', while the deputy at Greville considered that all development within the school should be linked to achieving and that her staff must have high standards because exam results had increased. She expressed a wish to 'continue to see, hopefully, an increase in exam success'. The headteacher of this school even included the standards of qualifications within his vision, saying, 'I suppose that the vision is also to ensure that students leave school with good qualifications.'

Standards of performance were also incorporated in the vision held by the leaders of Yarborough School, where the deputy headteacher reported that 'the vision has been to raise performance standards'. He also described how the headteacher always focused on achieving high standards: 'If you say to [the headteacher] some things about the community aspects of it and about these projects, he's like, yeah but what about standards. He is looking at how he can improve standards consistently.' This deputy referred throughout his interview to the Standards Agenda and levels of quality assurance. He illustrated how school leaders were influenced by the political aspects associated with accountability (TDA, 2009) and demonstrated that this focus on standards was embedded within the Senior Leadership Team.

A similar focus was evident at Blackwood School, where the deputy headteacher described how targets were used to monitor standards through ongoing tracking systems. The headteacher always encouraged high standards from the deputy by providing 'constructive feedback on where I could have done better, you know, in delivering or suggested ideas of how to improve'. Similarly, the Greville School deputy felt she was held accountable by the head for maintaining high standards; her performance was tracked and monitored through the Performance Management Systems. This was also the case for the deputy at Raleigh School, who knew that she was held accountable for high standards through the Performance Management Systems, as well as by the measures achieved in examination results. As Curtis (2008) maintains, accountability for the progress made by students in a school will be increased by much more regular information to parents, instead of just one final examination at the end of Key Stage 3. As the head of Raleigh School noted:

> currently the departments are debating what to do now that SATs has disappeared and how we are going to ensure quality control in terms of assessment; you know now that the external exam process is gone and what is going to replace that.

It was evident that staff at all levels were held accountable for maintaining and measuring high standards and, where external levels were not available, it was seen to be important that some internal method of measuring standards within the school should be in place.

Ofsted criteria coupled with examination results were used by the leaders of Raleigh School as external measures of standards. The Raleigh School deputy described the process by which the Senior Leadership Team responded to examination results and to Ofsted visits. She explained how they analysed their progress after receiving feedback from these sources and ensured standards remained high by making sure their reassessments were:

> aligned to the SEF, aligned to the school development plan taking shape and the departmental development plan being written. Largely in the summer term the leadership team will tend to meet together, either off site or on site, and have a look and share and discuss.

It can be seen that in this case the Senior Leadership Team was included in the process of maintaining high standards and felt accountable for achieving and maintaining them. As a group, the headteachers in this study referred to the need for the quality of education to be high. Indeed the headteacher of Yarborough School made references throughout his interview to this as a measure. He suggested that the progress made in the school should be considered in terms of quality learning experiences and explained how staff development needs to be about developing skills and expertise. This was also evident when the headteacher of Blackwood School discussed the difference that getting a quality education can make for young people – an opinion that was supported by the headteacher of Raleigh School, who justified the recent award of 'high performing specialist school status' based on the quality of its teaching in spite of the school's challenging circumstances. The same headteacher demonstrated an example of management-by-exception when he described how people within his school knew of the standards required, and stated that he would intervene if their behaviour or performance fell below the level he deemed to be acceptable.

It can be seen therefore that the headteachers' focus on maintaining and raising standards was achieved to a considerable extent by ensuring all teachers were held accountable for their allocated duties. Securing accountability is one of the National Standards for Headteachers, which set out the professional knowledge, understanding and attributes deemed necessary to carry out headship in the twenty-first century (DfES, 2004b). Most of the standards are derived from externally imposed criteria. The need to respond to these external criteria may be in large part responsible for headteachers acting as transactional leaders and having a focus on standards and external measures when leading their schools.

Looking to national standards: The use of external measures

The analysis of headteachers' focus on national standards is also linked to another indicator of transactional leadership, that of using external measures as a way of assessing the performance of schools. Such indicators show that headteachers were driven by transactional, extrinsic, measures as opposed to transformational, intrinsic, measures. Not surprisingly, many schools referred to the measure of five A* to C passes at GCSE. This is a nationally used method of judging the success of schools, based on the percentage of students who score a grade C or above in five subjects in the GCSE examinations, and is one of the measures used nationally to rank schools (Chartered Institute of Educational Assessors, 2009). This standard, if not met, is one of the external indicators that may lead to a school being classified as 'failing' by Ofsted. Blackwood School's deputy stressed the importance of students achieving five A* to Cs. Greville School's deputy described changes that had occurred in her school by referring to the performance of students against this external measure: 'In terms of student outcome, we've come from – in 2000 we were 15%, five A*s to C this year we were at 74%.'

This external measure is one that many school leaders strive to improve, although the methods by which they reached this improvement did vary. The deputy at Blackwood School described how the Senior Leadership Team had introduced a new course-work-based curriculum that guaranteed almost everyone who attended school regularly at least five A* to C grades. He explained that everyone in the school will follow 'a core curriculum which is Maths, English, science, DT because we are a technology college, PE because that's part of the curriculum and IT'.

Inevitably headteachers often used these external measures of indicators of improvement; the headteacher of Greville School anticipated that 'we will hopefully continue to see an increase in exam success and an increase in opportunities for our students', while the headteacher of Raleigh School reported that:

> English and Maths went up, the functional skills went up, the percentage A to Cs came down slightly, but actually more kids passed more things than they'd ever done before, and that was a great statistic to hang on to.

This evidence demonstrated how headteachers are now required to measure the performance of their pupils using quantitative, definable results in the form of examination percentages.

Both the headteacher and the deputy of Raleigh School also referred to the more subjective judgements provided by Ofsted. The latter explained how they reassessed their work based on exam results and Ofsted visits:

> There's always that tweaking process anyway after results come in because there has to be a response one way or another to what the results looked like. There was a response after Ofsted in 2006 and we are of course anticipating Ofsted again this new year coming so there are interim, you know moments where we have to stop and look and reassess.

The headteacher at Blackwood School also demonstrated that she refocused following Ofsted inspections. She stated that following a report from Ofsted, 'we need to ensure that all our lessons are good or outstanding'. When the Yarborough School head referred to the school's Ofsted inspection, the emphasis was on methods of measuring its impact in order to demonstrate how much the school had improved. He also noted the use made of other statistical information, including measures of the socioeconomic area, stating how these measures revealed the extent of social deprivation:

> I look at the social indexes factors; for instance in this school 38% of our students have lone parents, 51% live in the poorest 10% of housing stock in the country and 21% are on free meals. The indices of multiple deprivations are high and I think these issues have got to be tackled, the issues to do with child poverty.

This demonstrated the headteacher's use of external measures to identify his personal priorities and areas for intervention. While the headteacher of Greville School also used the external measure of the social deprivation of the area, he used it to identify that their statistical results were even more of an achievement. He quoted the measure of students who leave the school and are recorded as NEET (not in education, employment or training) as an external measure of success:

> We are very proud of things like our NEET figure, for example last year it was 0%, so there was no student from our year 11 who had a negative destination at all, which for the challenging community that we serve that's a massive indicator for improvement really.

The same head made references to the Government's *Every Child Matters* agenda (DfES, 2004a), discussed earlier as an external measure of success. He used it to judge the school to be successful. These external measures were supported by statistical percentages gathered from either questionnaires or exam results.

The deputy head of Yarborough School made reference to the National Challenge Advisor (NCA), an externally appointed consultant who works with the school to help set targets and identify improvements or opportunities for future improvements (DCSF, 2009). The SLT's awareness of these external measures is such a priority that they were willing to revise their Self-Evaluation Form (SEF) after consultations with the National Challenge Advisor. The deputy headteacher described this process in detail:

> We had the National Challenge Advisor in yesterday and he wanted to change our SEF judgments and basically said that if we don't change our SEF judgments he would actually put in his report, because of National Challenge like, that he would put in his report that he didn't agree with our judgments on certain things. What I said was okay, we'll change them, because we don't want a report going in that says NCA doesn't agree with it.

The degree to which external measures have become important to the success of schools is illustrated by their leaders being prepared to alter their internal judgements to ensure they are aligned with external measures.

The manner in which headteachers focused on the same criteria established by external bodies to deem the school successful was evidence that headteachers are influenced by the political environment in which they operate. Again, this is a national pressure imposed on all headteachers and is not specific to particular communities or authorities. Headteachers are concerned about published figures such as league tables and NEET figures and as such take on a transactional role, being concerned about external measures of success, rather than transformational, internal measures. This means that a headteacher's actions are often reactive and responsive to the findings of these external measures, and this was the next most frequently occurring aspect of transactional leadership traits.

Rearranging the priorities:
Reactiveness and responsiveness

Reactive and responsive actions are typical of transactional leadership (Bass and Riggio, 2006). Such actions were evident in all the schools and were often related to the findings provided by external measures. For example, the deputy from Raleigh School detailed how Ofsted could cause the school to become more responsive, based on their findings:

> We have had a couple of occasions where either Ofsted or responding to something like post-16 where the deadlines and timings of things have been out of our control can tend to slightly make us rethink our development plans. It doesn't deflect from the overall whole school priorities because they're fixed and the development planning cycle is fixed; you know that's on the calendar and that doesn't alter, that stays as it is. Where things may get blown slightly off course is perhaps in the prioritization of certain things happening in a certain time. Something may move to the top of the pile that would have been dealt with in a different way, but sometimes deadlines and timelines alter that are out of the school's control. Ofsted can throw up interesting things that you don't necessarily plan for.

This point was also made by the deputy from Blackwood School, who commented that the school was 'always going to have short-term urgent issues, and these are always things that you've got to deal with'. The deputy from the same school explained how he expected the school to be able to respond to issues and incorporates this into the long-term planning:

> I think as long as you plan for these things to happen within your planning of the week, you know that you can create capacity during that planning in that you can say, look there's going to be times where I'm going to be pulled out for a day through an investigation or because something else has happened. The key is that you always make sure that you've got the long-term vision, with a time-line of your different areas, so that you know you've got to hit those areas by that deadline and that it's not smooth running where you can just sit down in your office.

There is therefore an acceptance on the part of school leaders that part of their daily expectation is to react to changes that are unanticipated, and they acknowledge this by allocating free time for contingencies.

The deputy at Yarborough School explained that they responded to a request from the unions to ensure training was effective and not overly time-consuming:

> It is actually the Unions that have prompted us to do this because what they have said is they want to ensure that this session is being used effectively, which is a positive actually from the Union rather than the Union asking why we are doing this.

Here the school responded to the request by, in their view, actively reacting in order to prevent future issues. This practice is also shared by Greville School, where the headteacher detailed his pre-emptive approach to managing the school by incorporating reflective thinking into his daily practices: 'I think and look at things in a way that tends to minimize issues.' This practice of reflection and reaction in order to minimize future issues was also evident in other schools. The deputy headteacher of Yarborough School shared his concerns about previous attempts at communication within the community, explaining, 'We've not actually, I don't think communicated that effectively in the last few years. I think we've communicated it to the groups that needed to hear it.' He also described how, in response to this reflection, communication within the community has become a new priority for the school. The headteacher of Blackwood School explained how she felt that her actions were often a response to the particular circumstances of the school and noted her awareness that, as these circumstances change, she would have to react in a different manner: 'It can't continue to be like that and I think that's only because of the circumstances we are in, we have got a short amount of time to make a difference.'

In each school it was obvious that the headteacher had to be responsive and needed to be able to react to changing circumstances, especially in response to Ofsted or other external bodies and particularly if there was an early indication of falling standards. This is a feature of transactional leadership. The need to behave in a transactional manner is dictated, at least in part, by the political environment within which headteachers work. The feedback provided by Ofsted reports and examination results acted as a focus for headteachers and directed them to become more reactive and responsive. Their actions were influenced by the measures imposed upon them and by the priorities set elsewhere. They responded to this by becoming transactional and taking corrective measures to ensure, for example, that they matched Ofsted's definitions of a good school. However, these headteachers did not easily accept deviation from their plans.

The mechanistic school: Planning, reward and continuity

Transactional leaders tend to resist any deviation from predetermined plans, are reluctant to change anything quickly and see staff motivation as predominantly reward-driven. These factors all stem from the extent to which headteachers view their schools as mechanistic in nature, as opposed to being organic and constantly evolving (Bass and Riggio, 2006). When an organization is viewed as mechanistic and static, there is a perception that there is a desired blueprint which the organization should match. Accordingly, the implication is that deviation from the plan is erroneous and action should be taken to maintain the ideal model. This explains why transactional leaders do not accept deviation from their planned developments and are reluctant to make any quick changes.

When there is a preconceived plan for the organization, it is possible to identify whether actions are moving towards this, or away from it. Hence, rewards and punishments can be used to steer the development of the organization. This is an example of transactional leadership through management-by-exception, where leaders only become involved when they perceive a need to alter the behaviour of others as a possible means of achieving desired developments. Although the three indicators above were mentioned throughout the interviews, their influence was not as evident as those evidenced in the four preceding sections, and the low frequency of references implies that they were not as important to the headteachers as achieving tasks, maintaining standards, using external measurements or reacting to these external measures.

There was very little evidence in these schools that heads resisted the need to bring about change. This may have been because of the very nature of the situations in which the schools found themselves. However, although the headteacher of each school expressed the need to be responsive to change, there was evidence of a reluctance to modify existing plans. For example, the head of Raleigh School stated that he found the deviations to be annoying: 'If it didn't annoy me then I wasn't committed in the first place; sorry a simple equation, but I believe that.' There was also evidence of the reluctance of the headteacher of Blackwood School to deviate from her plans. This newly appointed headteacher brought practices from her previous school and it was clear that she intended to implement these without change. The timings of the school day were to be altered exactly to match her previous school, as was the offered curriculum content. She expressed a reluctance to change: 'I don't think I ever will deviate from that vision, because otherwise it is not worth the paper it's written on, is it?' This headteacher also described the leadership structure at her previous school and her intention to mirror it at the new school, including the entire line management structure and the method by which teams work together to ensure every leader has an understudy who is exposed to the systems in place. She claimed that this provides the capacity for staff to fill vacant positions whenever needed and explained that 'when a person leaves or the College expands, [then] somebody can slot up into another position and by doing this they need to be exposed to experience whole college issues, within that…particular initiative'. The implication is that this headteacher did not expect to deviate from her previous school's structure. She had no intention of allowing the staff to adopt roles which might be better suited to their individual skills and personalities, regardless of what that may bring to the school. At least in this respect, therefore, her stance was instrumental and transactional.

Transactional leaders utilize reward as their main method of motivation, and this can be achieved by providing praise or reprimands as psychological rewards (Kurland et al., 2010). Although this motivational method may have been used in the schools, there were very few references to it in the interviews with either headteachers or deputy headteachers. The only evidence came from Blackwood School, where the deputy referred to providing temporary contracts for specific tasks, which implied there are some financial incentives associated with the undertaking of a new project. The headteacher of this school explained how she judged effective staff development by movement into higher paid positions, such as Advanced Skills Teacher or Head of Department. However, it is also possible that these statements did not refer to utilizing reward as a method of motivation, but focused on developing people by moving them into new positions, thus providing the opportunity for them to expand their skills and experience and allowing them to gain exposure to a series of temporary projects that matched their current developmental requirements.

The other headteachers all felt that it was necessary to accept change. The headteacher of Yarborough School declared a strong belief in 'change management' and detailed great developments in the school structure, ethos, culture and beliefs. The head of Greville School agreed:

> In terms of changes with regard to ethos, and things like that I suppose over the past eight years or so both myself and the previous head have worked very hard on looking at changes in culture and belief and those kind of things and that has led to a significant improvement in terms of outcomes as well. So as well as the structural changes there's also been a kind of ethical change as well, you could say, within the school.

Similarly, the headteacher of Raleigh School supported this belief, particularly in respect of how essential it is to change. He revealed that he viewed his school as consisting of five different schools – one for each year group – each of which is, in his view, both independent of the other four and unique, requiring a range of individual initiatives that ensure that the school best suits its individual needs. The pride with which these headteachers described the changes they had brought to the school is significant, however, since it can be thought of as an indication that their preferred leadership style is not transactional, but rather is directed towards transformation.

Conclusions: Transactional leadership

The evidence presented in this chapter shows that all four headteachers who took part in the first research study demonstrated instances where they behaved as transactional leaders. Although some indicators were more evident than others, there is little doubt that the headteachers in every school undertook actions that can be identified as transactional. This was most evident in the case of the most recently appointed headteacher, but evidence was plentiful across all eight interviews. A point to note is that transactional leadership was more evident when headteachers were new to the post, and became less so as they gained experience of serving within this socially deprived area. It may be that as headteachers gain experience, they gravitate more towards transformational and less towards transactional, or it may be that the unique environments within which they work, where they serve a community of high social deprivation, cause this change to take place. Alternatively, it could be that new headteachers felt the need to change in difficult or unfamiliar circumstances and felt they had to do this by directing action, perhaps because they did not know where to place their trust. There was some evidence for the social area being responsible for this change; headteachers who had served in more than one school, and whose actions were still highly transactional when they arrived in Coalborough, became less transactional as they developed into the role of headteacher of a school serving a community with a high social deprivation index.

The extent to which a headteacher is transactional could, to a large extent, be attributed to external pressures and the levels of comparing and benchmarking schools that are in place, rather than to their preferred leadership style. The deputy at Greville School made a reference to this possibility when she described how the school used to be guided eight years ago, stating that they would not return results similar to those that they had previously achieved because of the nature of the new monitoring systems. She maintained that 'if we turned out 15% [grades A* to C at GCSE] this year, not only the local authority but Ofsted and various other people would be all over us'. This illustrates the levels of accountability felt by schools due to the external pressures from nationally set targets and Ofsted inspections. It is possible that transactional actions are ultimately influenced by political pressure, forcing headteachers to focus on external measures and national standards instead of on the personal development of people, where they would prefer to focus. Headteachers are encouraged to be responsive to political changes and are constantly using external criteria to compare themselves with others, with the real threat of being classified as a failing school if they do not meet these required standards. The nature of these demands for accountability through externally imposed criteria encourages headteachers to hold some measures as constant. These are priorities set by external agencies. Such measures prevent them from changing quickly or deviating from their long-term plans, even if they feel this would be more beneficial for their schools and their students. These external measures are in force for all schools, and as such do not necessarily reflect the nature or background of the unique schools within this study or of other schools in challenging circumstances. However, the level of high social deprivation experienced by these schools may be a factor influencing the level of transactional leadership that is taking place. Schools in such challenging circumstances may need to strive harder to meet national targets.

It is noticeable that transactional leadership actions are often associated with the day-to-day running of a school and the achievement of tasks, not with the growth and development of new educational movements, new ideas or of individual people. External political pressures hold headteachers accountable for achieving specific, measurable benchmarks. This prevents them from fully pursuing their own path for school development, causing them to focus on national agendas and developments identified by Ofsted inspections. However, these measurable outcomes may be better achieved when headteachers focus on the less tangible goals of motivating followers and developing individuals – in other words on leadership which might be termed transformational.

4

Using Transformational Leadership in Schools

In the previous chapter, it was shown how far headteachers in the main part of this study used transactional methods in their leadership of four schools in the challenging circumstances of Coalborough local authority. It was argued that this is mainly, although not exclusively, a response to externally set targets and externally determined policy and procedures. In this chapter, the extent to which these headteachers used transformational is explored.

Transformational leaders base their work on their core values which are expressed through a vision for the school. Such leaders are flexible, able to initiate and cope with change and are extremely person centred. One of the main points of focus for transformational leaders is their intention to develop and mentor followers, constantly nurturing optimism and enthusiasm throughout the school while empowering colleagues to do more than they ever expected they could do. The analysis in this chapter uses the seven main features of this transformational leadership that were illustrated in Table 2.3. These are presented in order, from most frequent incidences to least frequent, as a means of illustrating how often headteachers utilized these indicators across various aspects of their work.

Person-centredness: A key attribute

One of the strongest features of transformational leaders is that they are very person-centred (Albritton, 1995) and concentrate on developing others and empowering them to achieve. Of the seven actions deemed to reveal areas of transformational leadership, this characteristic was the most evident in the data collected from the headteachers in the main study. They consistently revealed that they have a belief in students and staff as people with great qualities. The head of Raleigh School described how he enjoyed developing others:

> I like making a difference for people. I've seen people, particularly being a coach on the 'leading from the middle' and things of that nature. I've seen people develop and come on.

A different example of belief in others, in this case students, was given by the head of Greville School, when describing his faith in the merits possessed by children: 'Young people get a really bad press and it's just not true, is it? I mean our students are, on the whole, well mannered, caring, brilliant kids.' The same view was evident when the headteacher of Blackwood School explained that: 'young people here are genuinely personable, and if you treat them with respect and are interested and involved in them, there's a real genuine interest to talk to you'. The deputy at Blackwood believed that:

> the students, the majority of students, the vast majority of the students are absolutely fantastic, absolutely fantastic. In fact I've worked in several schools and this is the best set of students I've ever known and quite surprising really, very, very, very pleasant. Will make eye contact with you, will say good morning, will interact with you in a conversation.

These statements illustrate a strong affinity to students as people, irrespective of examination performance or achievements within the school, a mindset that, as Anderson and Anderson (2001) point out, is an important feature of transformational leadership.

A belief in the qualities possessed by students was also echoed by the headteacher of Raleigh School when describing the benefits for teachers who attempt to motivate students. He demonstrated that he felt students' potential for achievement was limitless provided they could be motivated, saying that students will 'go through walls, they go through walls every week, that's the beauty of being here'. He expressed, in a recurring theme, how privileged he felt to be working in the school: 'I've been privileged enough to work with them and hopefully, bring people on as far as I can possibly influence it, that also is a great motivating factor for me coming in. I love what I do.'

The headteacher of Yarborough School also identified with this feeling of privilege and even compared his expectations for his students with those for his own children:

> I will fight for our kids, and I will fight for them in terms of that I want them to have the things that they haven't had in terms of quality learning

experience, and it disappoints me when I hear or read about negative stuff about kids in communities, kids in this, kids in that, and I value them all enormously, from the least to the most and I do that in terms of wanting for them and the things that I hope I'll give to my own children, and this is an interesting, and I think very pertinent, philosophy that I have. I say to the staff in both schools that I have the privilege to run, that I expect no less for the children here than I do for my own children in the schools I send them to, and I think that's a powerful statement in terms of what I want and what my expectations are.

This feeling of being privileged to work with children was shared by the deputy of Raleigh School when outlining her reasons for wishing to work in her school:

I've seen people develop and come on, you know not because of me, but I've seen that and I've been privileged enough to work with them and hopefully, you know, bring people on as far as I can possibly influence it, that also is a great motivating factor for me coming in.

Another aspect evident from the interviews with the leaders of the schools was the desire to ensure that students achieved personal success. Both the head and deputy of Greville School made several references to this, and the deputy described it as one of the original aims of the school: 'One of the founding aims of [the school] which hasn't changed along way is that students come, achieve and believe in themselves.' The headteacher reiterated this when he discussed his vision for the school:

Making sure that students enjoy school and that they feel safe and secure in school, and I suppose the vision is as well to ensure that students leave school with good qualifications but also as good citizens.

This headteacher's holistic view focused on students as valuable people, both in the employment arena and in the community. The deputy of Blackwood School also made reference to this aim, maintaining that 'it's about getting as many students to achieve as much as possible and to aspire to doing the best that they can so that they can have the best life that they can'. He continued to explain that achievement did not always mean academic qualifications, but could include other experiences: 'You know qualifications aren't the be-all and end-all of a school education, it is [about] the variety that is there.' The Greville School deputy head detailed some of the extra activities that students undertook:

One of the big things that we have done also is as well as the exam results. We try and give the kids an absolutely massive range of pastoral activities;

we do trips all over the place; there's hundreds of them go; they are going to Canada this year. But these are the large trips, but it is also about giving them the opportunity to look a little bit further than [Coalborough] and to raise their aspiration and realize there is a big world out there and that it is not just centred around [Coalborough], and I think that is our aim and goal to give these kids the best chance in life that we can.

The head of Blackwood School was also keen to introduce new experiences for students and encouraged them to make pledges of ten things to do before leaving school. One of these included taking part in an international visit in order to broaden their life experience.

Support for vulnerable students was also mentioned by the school leaders. At Greville School, the deputy thought that:

one of the things that we have been really good at is that the students who come from tough backgrounds actually come in and get an awful lot of support, they leave a lot of the baggage at the school gates and come in and feel quite secure and looked after.

Her equivalent at Blackwood was of the same opinion:

There are other students of course as well that have the social problems and again when … there's things here that we need to do for these students, it's not just about, you know, excluding them or kicking them out … this is something here that's really close to my heart that the vulnerable students in college, whether through behaviour or through social issues, are the people that we really need to look after and those people that we need to higher their self-esteem and get them through college with good qualifications, where they've got options when they're 16 and they're not going to be just left out in the cold.

A different theme that arose several times from the Blackwood School head was the desire to involve students more in their education within the school:

The other issue is students and using students in professional development and really recognizing that if we are serious about co-construction, and it's not just a buzz-word, that, if we are learning from each other all the time, we can learn from our students, and it's about making sure that student voice is real within our college.

This statement demonstrated the transformational view: that all people learn from each other and that students should be placed at the heart of the school as their opinions, views and values are recognized. These heads described the level of privilege they felt in being able to serve children from this socially deprived area. They not only focused on the externally measured aspects of schooling but also had a strong desire to provide students with a range of experiences that they were unlikely to receive without the school's input, such as enrichment activities and international experiences. This was closely linked to the process of developing and changing individuals and the schools themselves through staff involvement and participation.

The approaches to staff development by heads in the study also demonstrated aspects of transformational leadership. The head of Blackwood School recognized the importance of staff involvement when she said that 'without the whole staff it can't be done'. The Greville head also supported this approach:

> We have lots of forums where staff can raise ideas and challenge thinking and challenge the direction the school is going in as long as it's kind of very productive and positive and it's leading to improved outcomes, and I positively encourage that kind of debate and dialogue.

Indeed, this head made many references to the school ethos of involving and valuing staff, and asserted that: 'if you're involving staff comprehensively in the way you are trying to reach a vision and you're trying to lead a school into a particular direction, then that in itself is developmental'. Attempting to ensure that the staff felt valued and challenged was also one of the priorities at Greville. According to the headteacher:

> We've invested a lot time, energy and money. I suppose, in ensuring that staff do feel as if they are valued and that they are constantly being challenged both pedagogically and also with regard to their career progression

The deputy added:

> if people are given the opportunity to develop their skills, then that's when they're happy and content in where they are working and what they are doing, I think because, they have always got a new challenge.

Involving staff in school development was also considered to be very important at Yarborough School where, according to the head and deputy, respectively, 'staff are very much involved in the vision, [There is] a lot of work to be done in sharing and agreeing the values of visions' and 'we did a visioning day with all the staff as part of the training day, and we asked them to look at what would be their vision for the college and the community'.

Similarly, the deputy of Blackwood School described the support he had received from the headteacher and the methods she used to encourage him. He defined her approach as 'very intently supportive, and there's always a two-way dialogue, but it's also about letting me go and do what I need to do without too much interference, or very little interference to be honest', while the headteacher herself said that 'we as leaders recognize the talent that we've got and almost release that talent, so there's peer group learning, sharing good practice'. This approach was upheld by the Yarborough headteacher: 'It's very much about empowering and enabling people at all levels to succeed' and also by his colleague at Raleigh, who agreed that 'their energies are correctly channelled where they want to be, which is in teaching and learning, [. . . and] if the balance is right, it's a hell of a powerhouse'.

Headteachers also demonstrated faith in their staff when discussing the level of school leadership in place. The headteacher of Blackwood School believed that this is essential in order to be effective: 'My experience tells me that you can only be a totally effective leader, headteacher, with an effective team around you, and I really do believe that.' The head of Raleigh School demonstrated a similar commitment by expanding his leadership team to include new teachers, demonstrating the faith he has in the abilities of staff:

> We've now got a senior leadership team, but we've got a senior management team that's twice the size of the [original] senior leadership team . . . and a minority are long serving, half of them were either NQTs [Newly Qualified Teachers] when I came, or have been appointed since.

The person-centredness at the heart of transformational leadership was evidenced by the importance of trust and belief in the team shown by headteachers of other schools, including the Blackwood head:

> Trusting your team around you, and I mean trusting in every sense, trusting their qualities, trusting their skills, and you can't do it on your own, and I've seen that, you know in my experience of getting to this level, so it is about the team that you have around you, and I suppose as a good leader, it's about encouraging and recognizing those things in your team.

This trust was also demonstrated by her colleague at Yarborough School:

> There is not one person around that table that I am not confident that they can do their job, and I think that's the key aspect of [the headteacher's] leadership, and what he's [provided is the] . . . ability for us to continue to evolve and develop as a college, because we have got the individuals who can do that.

The headteacher of Raleigh School pointed out that he was attempting to increase this level of self-belief and the deputy headteacher described how some staff were still in the initial processes of developing confidence:

> There's a lack of confidence amongst one or two of them, to really go for it, and they still feel the need to come and check that everything is fine, that they're afraid of making a mistake so there is still work to do, in taking that fear factor out of that process, so it's not entirely there, the intention is there; certainly with some people, it has sunk in, and they are beginning to run with things that they would ordinarily have felt the need to check on every five minutes.

The level of headteachers' trust in their deputies' abilities was demonstrated by the deputy of Yarborough School, who declared that '[the headteacher] gave me that freedom to do whatever I wanted and he gave me the opportunity'. The Blackwood School deputy head shared his experience of being developed by the headteacher:

> I don't see myself by any means as a finished product, I've got to keep developing, but I'd also like to keep moving up as well, and I feel that I can do that now. Whether I thought that I could do that two years ago to how I feel now, and the difference and the transformation in myself and my own development has been quite amazing because I don't think that I would have ever of thought that I would have been in this position.

The development of leaders was also seen as a priority for the headteacher of Greville School: 'The general spirit I think of leadership is that we are looking to create leaders, develop leaders and find leaders, wherever they are.' According to the deputy of Yarborough School, the headteacher had created 'a collective approach, so that we work together', adding that 'I've always been confident and comfortable in my position in school, and he's instilled that in me'. The headteacher's ability to see the potential leadership skills in staff has resulted in his willingness to

> move people into positions, into promoted positions that at first you might have thought, am I ready for this? But I think what he is good at is spotting potential, putting you in place and letting you make mistakes, but then supporting you in those mistakes as well.

This headteacher's belief in people was evident here and is demonstrated by his willingness to cope with and accept any mistakes arising from providing staff with new opportunities and challenges, accepting it as part of the development process that staff will go through as they move into these positions of leadership.

The headteacher at Greville School recognized leadership at every level in his school:

> I feel that everybody's got a stake, everybody's a leader whether it's students, your cleaners, your kitchen staff, your deputy head, your head of department, your caretaker, everybody's got a stake, haven't they? Everybody leads, everybody sets examples, and that's the way that is the best way in my opinion.

The heads' underpinning belief in people, therefore, is independent of their role or experience and relates to individuals and the qualities they possess. The head of Blackwood School similarly stressed her excitement and enthusiasm at the notion that leadership is not just top-down. This belief in people, and the ability to match people to roles suitable to an individual's potential, was reported by deputies to be one of the main attributes of the headteachers; at Yarborough, according to the deputy head, 'in eight years, [the headteacher] has put together a team of individuals who are all happy in their positions, who are all motivated in their positions'.

The relationships that have been formed with parents and the community members are areas that also demonstrated the headteachers' focus on people. It is vital to headteachers that the community is involved in the future direction of the school, as this will be beneficial to the learning experiences of students (Leithwood and Jantzi, 2009). The headteacher of Greville School explained how they were moving towards Specialist Trust Status because of the involvement with parents and the community:

> It's been the whole community really; both parents, students, governors, partners of the school, have all been involved in creating that vision, that ethos, for change and for improvement, and I think by doing this is what's led to the trust really. The establishment of a cooperative trust in the school is what we need to galvanize the whole community into feeling that it has a stake and a part to play in driving these improvements forward. So in that sense, I really do feel that it is a very comprehensive shift; it's not just one group of stakeholders, or me, or a leadership team who have actually been involved in that, it has been a comprehensive plan of action.

The headteacher of Yarborough School also shared this desire to involve the whole community in the development of the school:

> It's about more partners in the vision, understanding what the benefits are to them and then how you go about doing that and clearly you've got to

involve all staff, you've got to involve students, you've got to involve their parents, you've got to involve governors and by doing that, you necessarily involve the wider community and other stakeholders in your organization whether it be those who are education stakeholders, partners and or a deeper and wider community who are included, for instance student councils.

When the headteacher of Raleigh School discussed the community, he expressed an appreciation for the level of diversity of the wider community and an understanding that the contribution from the community was able to lead to improvements for all. He said that there is a

> multiplicity of communities, and I think that's a strength, because I don't think anyone should dominate another, and I don't believe that your geographically most, close physical community should dominate what you do . . . It should be a major player in it, but it should be a player in it, and the leavening you get from all those other communities makes it better for everybody.

This community involvement theme was also shared by the headteacher of Blackwood School who was keen to involve parents and community members in the education of students. She believed that this would lead to a better experience for students, as the community helps to shape the vision for the school. The head of Greville School had already started a process of involvement and had

> done some quite interesting work on engaging parents, and over a year ago now I actually wrote to parents and invited them to a visioning session that involved a real range of parents as well as some of our most difficult parents I suppose you could say, the hard to reach parents, across to parents who have been very supportive in the past, I wrote to them specifically inviting them up to school.

Throughout their interviews, all the headteachers described their belief in people and how they value the contributions that can be made by everyone. The headteacher of Yarborough School described himself as being 'passionate about people' and illustrated this when he talked about the levels of hope he saw within the community. He said that he was distressed by

> the levels of poverty, and not just economic poverty but social poverty as well in terms of families, in terms of their aspiration and in terms of their expectations and yet, what I also see in every bit of our community is

hope. I do believe that the vast majority of people don't want to be trapped inside with some of the negativity, which they portray but that they don't know how they're going to get out of where they are at. I think schools, if they are to become the heart of the communities, have the key role to play in challenging and changing the culture of communities and improving the aspiration, attitudes and values of the people who are currently perhaps disenfranchised.

He went on to describe himself as a 'missionary who feels privileged to be involved in shaping young people's lives'. He wanted to make schools in deprived areas friendlier places, where people can really flourish: 'I believe that a lot of our schools have got to become kinder places in terms of how we speak to each other and what our expectations are.'

A commitment to helping and improving people was also evident at Greville School, where the deputy explained that the most important thing she had learned from the head was to have belief in people. This sentiment demonstrated the degree to which a headteacher could be considered to be person-centred and provides evidence that the headteacher took a key role in developing and changing people. Throughout the interviews, headteachers revealed a trust and belief in their staff and an intention to build self-confidence and facilitate wide involvement in future developments for the school.

Development and change: Possibilities for people and their environment

Transformational leaders often see possibilities for others of which the people themselves are unaware. Bass and Riggio (2006) note how this feature of transformational leadership often enables people to achieve much more than with any other leadership style. This was the second most dominant recurring theme expressed by headteachers in this study, who were continually seeking to develop and change both the people they are in contact with and the environment within which they operate. The following comments sum up this sentiment: 'the more time you spend in the teaching profession, the more you see it as a way to bring about change' (Greville School Head), 'I need to recognize that changes have to be made in a short space of time, and actually getting on and doing it' (Blackwood School Head), and finally, in the opinion of the Yarborough School headteacher: 'There is a need for headteachers to get into change management processes; we've got to get into strategies of change...if you're not into change management and if you're not into thinking differently then perhaps you don't succeed.'

There is, however, a difference of emphasis here. While the head of Greville School saw positive opportunities for change, the heads of both Blackwood and Yarborough Schools saw change as a necessity without necessarily welcoming it. Part of the change process for some of these schools was the move from traditional school into the national programme of specialist colleges. This government initiative offers additional funding and an affiliation with a network of schools whose focus is to raise achievement. To join this affiliation, headteachers had to provide evidence that they had the potential to improve educational standards and could also form strong relationships with the communities which they serve (SSAT, 2009). The Greville School head referred to this change when he explained:

> The other changes I suppose and big changes in recent times have been that we have become a specialist school, a technology college. As a result of this and the success that we have had as a school, we then became a mentor school and then a consultant school, and most recently the biggest change has been that we are, from January the 1 2009, becoming a foundation trust school.

Similarly, the head of Raleigh School expressed his pride in securing an engineering specialism: 'We are part of the engineering specialist schools community; now that is a belter, born out of adversity; there are still only 60, six years in, there were precisely eight when we joined.'

All of the schools in the first part of this study had been accredited with specialist status by the time this research was carried out. However, each headteacher seemed to regard the most significant change as that which related to the school culture and ethos. The head of Blackwood School stated that she was 'about creating culture and ethos and mission'; a claim was also made by the head of Greville School:

> With regard to ethos, and things like that, I suppose over the past eight years or so both myself and the previous head have worked very hard at looking at changes in culture and belief and those kind of things, and this has led to a significant improvement.

This change in ethos occurred because of

> relationships across the board. I think that the relationships between staff and students, relationships amongst staff, relationships with parents, all of these things are absolutely critical really, in terms of improvement.

At Yarborough School, the headteacher considered the change in ethos to be his greatest achievement:

> I think the biggest change has been cultural change. By changing the culture of the organization, you are able to improve it more rapidly, and it's still, I think, a clear future at getting with some strategic planning about what could be achieved and how it's going to be done.

Other more tangible alterations described during the interviews included modification of the curriculum, where leaders from each school mentioned adjusting the curriculum to offer alternative courses that better met the needs of their learners, and the implementation of alternative approaches to teaching and learning. References were often made to the engagement of children in lessons and alternative methods of delivery within the classroom, such as providing a variety of learning experiences or bigger blocks of time that allow learners to become immersed in projects. The deputy at Yarborough School described the impact of making changes to the curriculum and its delivery as 'fantastic'. Each headteacher highlighted the need for more changes to assure the future success of the school. The head and deputy of Yarborough School planned to introduce social and emotional aspects of learning (SEAL) into their school. The deputy explained how important this could be for staff as well as for students:

> Developing the social and emotional aspects of learning the SEAL stuff and one of the key things we think for us is that our staff need it before the children do, because our staff don't know sometimes how to interact with the community that we serve, because a lot of them don't come from a community that is the same as this.

The leaders of Blackwood, Raleigh and Greville Schools wanted to create more leaders at all levels throughout their schools, with the view that this would help implement change more quickly. Transformational leadership has a strong focus on developing people to become more than they believe they can be. This leads to the creation of more leaders, as well as a greater synergy between staff and the contributions they make. The deputy at Blackwood School pointed out the benefits, including the importance of having more members of the school contributing to the development of new initiatives in order to bring about change:

> We're always looking for change, and we're always open to work with staff because I haven't and the other senior leaders haven't got a monopoly on good ideas. If we work together, co-construct with the students,

co-construct with the staff, it means that the college then has ownership because everybody's involved in it as opposed to it just being one person's vision.

Concerns relating to the level of the future sustainability of these changes were raised by this deputy headteacher, who identified this as a major priority when initiating improvements. Throughout every interview, it was apparent that in every school the role of the headteacher was to drive the school forward, using a process of identification and implementation of change. All the headteachers were transformational in the manner in which they attempted to develop individuals and influence the ethos of the school.

All four schools had adopted the government initiative and had become a Specialist College, allowing them to tap into a network of additional resources and funding that could enable them to achieve their desired changes more quickly. This factor may link to the community where these headteachers operated, in that without quick changes and additional resources many students would pass through the school without experiencing the level of entitlement the headteachers felt they deserved. The role of the headteacher in acting as an agent for change is a trait of transformational leadership and is strongly linked to the vision-focused aspect of transformational leadership.

Forming the future: The focus on vision

The ability to see a possible, improved future and to share this vision with others is a leadership skill that Hartog (2003) identifies as transformational, to the extent that it can motivate colleagues. This ability was evident in all interviews, and every deputy and headteacher could describe their vision for their school. These visions focused on raising both standards and the aspirations of students by ensuring students were at the centre of the processes implemented within the school. Examples of these were apparent in the interviews. The head of Greville School commented that 'the vision is really to ensure that we raise aspirations, and we raise achievement for all young people, and we do that by hopefully looking at how we can meet their individual needs'.

A similar sentiment ran through the head of Yarborough School's vision, which is

focused on young people first and foremost, and how we can enable and empower them to become successful adults, and how they can become the change managers; not just for their own futures but in terms of the credibility of schools as they become the next generation of parents. What

I mean by this is that we currently have generations of parents who have pretty poor experiences in our school and de facto have instilled these in their children. I think that's probably the factor for all schools in the areas where the socioeconomic conditions are less favourable.

The head of Yarborough School expressed a view that where there are poor socioeconomic conditions, the context of the school plays an important role in the creation of a vision, and the head of Blackwood School agreed indirectly, comparing the community to a smaller scale example of how education is being used to change the circumstances of underprivileged communities in South Africa:

The difference that you know that you can make when young people get a quality education is the only way that, over generations, South Africa is going to change. Now I actually believe that on a sort of national scale, this is relevant to small communities as well, and I suppose that actually takes me all the way back to my vision and my passion about why we do it. So my vision for this school is that all the decisions that are made, all the procedures, everything that goes on in the classroom, the corridors and everything, is about asking that question, how does this benefit every young person?... The decisions we make, everything we do, is about putting students first, [and] my vision is about realizing the potential of every child in this school.

A separate point made by every headteacher was the importance of the requirement that this vision be shared by others. The head of Blackwood School noted that: 'if we as leaders don't really encourage every member of staff to share that vision, it is not going to happen'. This point was also made by the head of Yarborough School:

It's about more partners in the vision, understanding what the benefits are to them and then how you go about doing that and clearly you've got to involve all staff, you've got to involve students, you've got to involve their parents, you've got to involve governors and by doing that, you necessarily involve the wider community and other stakeholders in your organization whether it be those who are education stakeholders, partners and or a deeper and wider community who are included, for instance student councils.

This headteacher also described how to achieve such a shared vision by creating and relaying a consistent future image that would become associated with the message, stressing the importance that message being consistent:

'I think it's about being consistently on message and it's what you do, not just in terms of what you say but how you say it.' He believed that the vision must be underpinned by the leader's personal values and implied that his role was to not only create the vision but also instil these values in others:

> Staff are very much involved in the vision. I think the vision has to emanate from the leadership, the leader of the school and it comes I think from their own personal beliefs and values, but if it's not something that is shared, then people don't buy into it and I think in that respect, there's a lot of perhaps coaxing, mentoring and a lot of work to be done in sharing and agreeing the values of visions.

Another feature of this focus on vision was the headteachers' belief that their vision was not yet complete. According to the Raleigh School head, it was still work in progress: 'there's still a way to go with some staff to see that delivering their sessions effectively actually is the best job they can do to help their colleagues in the school, because the kids then have total confidence'.

This headteacher proceeded to describe an alternative future for the school, one where he needed to step aside and let someone else take the school to even greater heights. The belief by the current headteacher that the agenda for the school would change and eventually outgrow him was, in his view, not only inevitable but also beneficial for the school. Interestingly, the head of Yarborough School also discussed his future plans and the route he could see himself following after leaving the school: 'I could make a contribution in terms of coaching, mentoring, empowering what I hope would be a new breed of headteacher and supporting them particularly in the emotional aspects of their job'.

Both headteachers, therefore, believed that their schools needed to continue to develop and that this might be facilitated, in future, by their successors. This is evidence that headteachers linked their personal values with the desire to develop and improve others, focusing on the sustainable development of their school rather than their present role. While this is a trait of transformational leaders, in this study the headteachers had an even stronger focus on developing young people than adults. They showed the desire to develop staff and community members, but they wanted to also instil in these adults a desire to empower the young people within their school, as well as to focus on raising the aspirations that these students had. This may be because the headteachers felt that students from a deprived background require additional intervention to raise their aspirations, in order to create a desire in them to escape from this level of deprivation. Not only did headteachers create a vision based on their personal beliefs and values, but also felt it was important that others shared this vision, that they felt a part of it and that they could play a significant role in seeing it come to fruition. This required transformational leaders to be inspirational.

Sharing the vision: Inspiring others

According to Armstrong (2004), transformational leaders are inspirational in their dealings, creating a desire in others to achieve more and to drive themselves forwards. The importance of this was highlighted by the headteacher of Blackwood School who explained that: 'we've got to be as inspirational as we can; I have to be...because there are some tough times ahead in terms of changes that have to be made'. She pointed out the importance of involving staff in order to achieve this level of motivation and to 'let them see that we are willing to take on their ideas'. The involvement of staff was also mentioned by the headteacher of Greville School, who found staff involvement to be the most effective way of communicating with staff:

> We consult with staff, we have staff questionnaires, we have those forums where staff can raise issues about how they feel their own personal development is going and professional learning is going. I think there are lots of opportunities for staff to actually feed back, and obviously we are constantly looking for opportunities as well which I think is crucial, I think about what it is that is going to move the institution further, who are going to be the key people to do that, sometimes that's driven by staff and sometimes it's driven by others.

The view that staff can feel inspired by being part of an establishment that is improving and has faith in them as individuals was also evidenced by the same head: 'People feel that we are a school that is moving forward, that's prepared to take risks, you won't be discouraged from taking risks and it's positively encouraged really.' Similarly, the deputy at Blackwood School noted that: 'we've started development because a couple of members of...young staff with three, four years' experience are now starting to deliver five, ten minute presentations on things that they are leading on'. The Greville School deputy explained that the headteacher had encouraged a high proportion of staff to take the NPQH (National Professional Qualification for Headship) at a very early stage in their career, which could be seen as expressing faith in staff and in their ability to achieve promotion in the future.

Another common factor in the data from the main study was references to the level of motivation. The deputy of Yarborough School described himself and the rest of the Senior Leadership Team as highly motivated, stating that 'not one of them is money motivated and I think because they see now that they have a voice and they have a say I do think it's the drive to them wanting to be involved'. The deputy head at Greville School concurred, describing colleagues as 'highly motivated staff, I think and I include myself in that as well, and again I think that's because we work very closely and collectively as a team'.

Perhaps the most revealing aspect of the inspirational aspect of transformational leadership was the deputies' belief that they were able to make a difference. The deputy of Raleigh School described how she had now been provided with a level of trust that filled her with confidence and was now sure that she could make a difference. She enjoyed 'making a difference, [and] the fact that [she has] some autonomy and some power to change things'. This view was shared by other school deputies, for example at Yarborough: 'I think it's about the old phrase of making a difference but, I think in this school it's true'.

Evidence that the deputies in all the schools felt they were empowered and capable of making a real difference to the school in which they work shows the degree to which headteachers in these schools created an environment where staff felt they were contributing to the future of the school, and played a significant role in shaping the futures of others. This empowerment of individuals can have a profound transformational effect on an organization (Albritton, 1995). Headteachers within these schools acted as transformational leaders as they not only wanted to change and improve the current situation, but also aimed to help others to know that they are also capable of achieving and that they could also make a significant difference. However, given the nature of the challenges facing the heads and deputies in these schools, these school leaders had to be fluid and flexible in their approach to both processes and outcomes by seeking and taking opportunities that offered themselves.

Seizing the chance: Fluidity and flexibility

Harris (2003) pointed out how transformational leaders have a high level of faith in human nature and often allow circumstances and personalities to play a part in the evolution of organizations in new, unforeseen directions. These unexpected developments can lead to paradigm shifts and improvements that could not have been anticipated or predicted. During the interviews, there were very few examples that could be categorized as evidence that the newly appointed headteacher of Blackwood School adopted a fluid and flexible approach, which may imply that she was reluctant to exercise this level of transformational leadership within her new school, as it involved taking risks. Here, the headteacher's only real evidence of flexibility is in the timings associated with her vision:

The methods by which I achieve that vision, the deadlines, the timings may have to change, so I'm not to get frustrated and impatient with people. I need to recognize that sometimes practical situations may mean that it can't happen then, or that particular thing can't happen, so I might have to just adapt it and compromises may have to be made along the way, but students will always come first in that compromise decision. Priorities may have to change, but I've got to keep the vision, because otherwise it will all just crumble. Won't it?

The headteacher of Yarborough School, on the other hand, revealed an acknowledgement of the need for leaders to be flexible:

I think we've got to be very much reviewers in our lives, and we've also got to be strategic thinkers and very objective thinkers, and I think one of the things which is critical in terms of what we do is how we handle situations and see what stops you in your track because I think that's an appropriate issue.

He also discussed the need for school leaders to be good managers of change, maintaining that headteachers need to get into change management processes and understand the strategies of change. The deputy disclosed that the headteacher allowed people to make mistakes and supported them, knowing he could always work with the staff to develop them whilst rectifying these mistakes. He characterised the head's attitude as very much 'let's do it and then worry about the processes separately', demonstrating confidence in his ability to adapt to the situations that may arise from this approach, a trait that Anderson and Anderson (2001) identify as being transformational. However, his deputy at Yarborough was not as comfortable employing this approach:

Sometimes I think we've jumped into a thing too quickly in a certain way and then we've had to go back and change it slightly, and I think what we have to do as an organization is to start to slow down a little bit at times.

The leaders of Raleigh, Yarborough and Greville Schools emphasized the importance of seeking others' views and consulting them. This would seem to support a desire to demonstrate a level of flexibility within their future plans. As the head of Greville School explained:

We've got a lot of distributive leadership in the school. We have lots of forums where staff can raise ideas and challenge thinking and challenge the direction the school is going in as long as it's kind of very productive and positive and is leading to improved outcomes. I positively encourage that kind of debate and dialogue.

He also found feedback crucial to ensuring the school moved forward, a view that was also demonstrated at Raleigh School, where the deputy described how staff play a part in deciding the future of the school through open discussion: 'It is done through all these different levels, lots of open discussion and people make their recommendations.' She also described how, in her opinion, the staff were able to adapt quickly to situations:

> We're not like a huge tanker that takes five miles to stop. We can adapt quite quickly; I don't think it used to be that way, but I think we have got better at adapting quite quickly to change and I think part of the reason we can do that is because our leadership team has become larger. When it was a smaller leadership team with people with very defined and specific job roles, it was sometimes harder to get people out of those, sort of out of that track they were in to then shift them and deviate them onto something else.

The headteacher of Raleigh also demonstrated a flexible approach to staffing and developing the school. He argued that he had re-invented the school several times whilst he had been in post and was pleased to have high levels of diversity throughout. He was sufficiently flexible to accept that the school mission statement was interpreted differently by different members of staff:

> We have one mission, but it can be interpreted differently in MFL [Modern Foreign Languages], catering, creative and performing, sport, wherever. Same thing, but this is how it looks over here guys and it'll be interesting to see where we go next.

He exemplified this belief in diversity several times. For example, when describing how the school operated he stated that: 'If you were to pick a random member of staff and ask them for a good exposition of what the school is about, you will find diversity'. He considered the school staff to be distinct and unique. All schools, in his opinion, were built on different personalities, different requirements and different skills. He described the benefits to Raleigh School of encouraging flexibility and ensuring that different perspectives work together in harmony:

> It's the interaction of different styles and the evolution of people who used to work one way and now quite clearly are working another, that keeps it, that leavens the place. I need the different approaches stitched

together, bumping into each other, not conflicting but bumping, bumping in and getting energy off each other and that's a good thing. I hope we've got a pretty fair example of most anyone you can think of in the building, you know we've got the rampant optimists, the absolute stone bottom pessimists, the technically gifted, the technically inept who will muddle through, the massively pupil centred, possibly too much, the massively staff centred, the massively subject centred, yeah, keep rolling I could probably, you know if you gave me one I could tell you, and it's not chaos, it's not even organized chaos it's constructive diversity.

This statement highlighted the headteacher's level of flexibility, showing he was able to accept and encourage high levels of diversity without feeling the need to rein them into a preconceived model of his school. The same headteacher also observed that his relationship with the community had differed significantly in each school he had worked in, since different communities had completely different requirements. He also revealed an enjoyment of entering into the unknown and described how many circumstances had made him reassess his approach; this reassessment would often lead to an improvement in the level of planned outcomes. This acceptance of the unknown and confidence in being able to adapt to it was summarized in the Raleigh School headteacher's statement about his plans for moving the school forward, which demonstrated flexibility in allowing the staff enough freedom to evolve naturally to some extent: 'We've done all this good stuff so what's next then? We think we know. It'll be interesting to find out.' Hence, Raleigh School was still evolving, changing and, it is to be hoped, improving.

The headteacher of Greville School also demonstrated a similar ability to evolve and adapt to an uncertain future. He explained how he encouraged all staff to take risks and was always looking for innovative initiatives. He described how he adapted to different situations and the importance of reading and interpreting situations to ensure that his actions match them, claiming that he used 'different styles of leadership to suit different contexts or situations as well as sometimes having to operate in an autocratic way, sometimes you don't, but it depends on the context really'. Here again this headteacher was, therefore, fully aware of the need to be flexible and was prepared to alter his actions to meet this need.

Across all the schools in the main study, it was evident that headteachers were able to maintain a level of flexibility that allowed staff to develop and contribute. Staff were encouraged to take risks, and the level of diversity across schools was seen as a strength to be celebrated. This accords with Jacobs' (2007) description of transformational leaders being confident enough to allow the school to grow through uncertainty and to view this as an opportunity to move forward. This flexibility of transformational leaders is centred in their approach and daily actions. Their core values, however, are a significant and permanent feature of how these headteachers approach their work.

Core values: A cornerstone of transformational leadership

Transformational leadership is linked to a strong purpose and a set of core values (Anderson and Anderson, 2001). The importance of headteachers' core values was established in two ways: firstly, by how headteachers referred to their core values and secondly, how they sought to relay these core values to others. Elements of the headteacher's core values were evident when the head of Greville School talked about his belief in young people, and his desire to ensure that his actions met their individual needs. He described how grateful he was to be in a position where he could do this, explaining 'I'm very proud to serve the communities I do, predominantly working class communities but with real aspirations to improve'. The headteacher of Blackwood School also discussed the desire to meet the needs of the individual and the importance of equal opportunities, maintaining 'I am passionate in every sense about equal opportunities in everything that that means'.

Their view was shared by the head of Raleigh School, who explained how he saw the diversity of the community as a real strength and aimed to support each individual by ensuring he meets their needs. When describing the importance of achievement, he related this to the needs of the students, pointing out that this was his reason for striving for improvement: 'It's still about maximizing what we do, we are about all the kids'. These statements reveal some aspects of the headteachers' core values of respect for others and a belief that people can achieve. The deputy of Yarborough School's view was that a headteacher fosters relationships based upon honesty, and that this is partly responsible for him being so successful. The head of the same school gave an insight into his personal values, describing how his belief in children helped to drive him forward:

> I will fight for our kids, and I will fight for them in terms of that I want them to have, the things that they haven't had in terms of quality learning experience, and it disappoints me when I hear or read about negative stuff about kids in communities, kids in this, kids in that as I value them all enormously.

This headteacher also revealed his determination to ensure that he was true to his values, even in the face of the adversity and external pressures that he considered may have prevented him from making the changes that he knew were needed: 'I think you have to be pretty bold and pretty determined to stand up for what you believe in when those constraints or shackles are repeatedly there.'

The head of Greville School also noted that it was just as important to him to ensure that students became good citizens as it was to ensure that they achieve academic results. Similar views were expressed by his colleagues at Blackwood and Yarborough schools. The headteacher of Yarborough said it was about 'first and foremost...how we can enable and empower them to become successful adults'. He also highlighted the need to develop self-respect, self-esteem and self-worth in individuals – the same point that was made by the deputy of Blackwood School. The headteachers of Greville and Yarborough schools went a step further, implying that their ultimate goal was to improve the moral stance of society; as the former explained: 'the impact that you can have is immeasurable in how you can change people's lives for the better and improve society and so I think [I came into teaching for] very noble reasons really'.

Similarly, the head of Yarborough School argued that schools have a 'key role to play in challenging and changing the culture of communities and improving the aspiration, attitudes and values of the people'. The interview evidence demonstrates that headteachers were driven by values and a desire to share these values with others, both to improve the lives of their pupils and to strengthen their local communities. The headteachers within this study all revealed considerable respect for others and a determination to provide learners with opportunities to raise their self-esteem and self-belief. They demonstrated a genuine care for students as individuals, and a desire to meet their individual needs and ensure that they received the same opportunities as others.

The strength of these values could explain why the headteachers in this study were so passionate about providing opportunities for students within this local authority. The idea that their students came from a socially deprived background conjures up a deficit notion of them as learners, coupled with a view that the students are not receiving the same benefits as other students. This in turn encourages these headteachers to provide more for their students in an attempt to remedy this situation and to ensure that a level of fairness is achieved. As well as meeting students' needs, the headteachers also wanted to help students to focus on self-development, enabling them to change. This fundamental belief of transformational leaders, that people can change, was held by headteachers and applied not only to others but also to themselves: the heads demonstrated that they were themselves still continually seeking to grow and change.

Developing people: The ability to change

The belief in core values and the ability to develop further have also been identified as traits associated with transformational leadership (Anderson and Anderson, 2001). Perhaps because of this, the headteachers in this study saw themselves both as leaders of change because of the challenging circumstances of their schools and as leaders who change because of the impact on them of their work. Evidence of the way in which headteachers change over time was provided by the deputy head of Raleigh School, who stated that:

> initially around the time that I was appointed I would say, it was fair to say that the head would have led most of those you know visions, those strategic visions were his, those strategic intents if you like were his, but very much shared by the governors and the senior leadership team as it was constituted then. Since then we've had a series of meetings and off site weekends away and that sort of thing, not just as a leadership team but with some of these extended leaders, middle leaders, who have come into the mix and we've gone off site to plan to look at the vision afresh.

This shift in movement from the headteacher acting independently from the rest of the school's leadership team to becoming a leader who involves an extended team was also noted by the deputy of Yarborough School:

> He's getting better [the headteacher]. A perfect example of it would be that he wants to still have three separate lunches coming into this year, and the leadership said no we don't want them. At one stage he said, this is an executive decision and I am saying it is three lunches, but he actually backed down when he said, right I'll listen to your idea and by the end of the year we'd actually changed it to two lunches. Four years ago, he would have never done this because it was he who was leading. He's started to realize that he has the capacity now underneath him to be able to pull away and just leave it and let it run.

The headteacher of Raleigh School echoed this when he discussed his belief that he needed to keep re-inventing himself to ensure that he still had something to offer to in the school:

> You can keep re-inventing yourself, or you can significantly re-invent yourself a reasonable number of times. Why I do this job still is that I still think the agenda. We haven't finished what I came to do. There will be a point where

we will finish what I came to do, and it is incumbent on me to get the hell out of the way at the right point, because the place is going to succeed again and will re-invent itself with somebody else. Somebody else, totally a new educational landscape, new challenges, brilliant technology, BSF [Building Schools for the Future], whatever, it will re-invent itself again or die.

The headteacher of Blackwood School also described how she used personal reflection as a means of checking and altering her actions, stating that she consciously tried to change her actions by relating them to her own role model: 'My father was a very successful man who was full of humility and a good moral man and I try, in everything that informs me, to have him as my role model.'

The head of Yarborough School mentioned that he actively sought to learn from external examples of good practice. He talked about his observations of foundation schools and academies and expressed his opinion that there was always something he could learn from sharing good practice in other schools, revealing that he was open to change and seeking ways to improve. Another headteacher, at Raleigh School, described how discussions with staff could produce changes in his beliefs:

I won't ask them to take an agenda forward unless I believe in it. I won't do it. There are things from the National Agenda that we do less of than other people might want us to do because I remain unconvinced, but I won't ask them to do it until I am. They can convince me. You know that play can change because they can convince me, I'm happy with that, but I hope they accept my view. I believe they accept that when we do things, I do it with them, not to them.

This head, like his three other colleagues and the four deputies in the main part of this study, was aware of the need to change and improve. None of them expected to maintain their present mode of operation, even if it had previously been successful. Moreover, the willingness to reflect and adapt was still linked very strongly to their values and beliefs, a characteristic of transformational leaders.

Conclusions: Transformational leadership

The evidence presented in this chapter has shown how all the headteachers in the study deployed transformational leadership within their schools, especially when developing people and moving the school forward. The use of transformational leadership rests heavily on the core values of these headteachers, all of whom were keen to produce opportunities for both students and staff to grow as individuals. The headteachers in this study accepted the need to be fluid and flexible, with a confidence that radiates from the transformational belief that people will always rise to the challenge and triumph over unexpected circumstances. In each school, the headteachers provided evidence that they helped others to share in the vision so that together they could be more than they currently were, creating an empowered, proactive approach.

The headteachers also showed a desire to create radical shifts in culture, behaviour and mindset that would be long-lasting and sustainable, which is a key feature of transformational leadership (Anderson and Anderson, 2001). These headteachers did not view themselves as people who had nothing more to learn. They were constantly growing and improving, in line with the nature of transformational leadership. Included in this personal development was the extent and nature of their use of transformational leadership which increased the longer they had been in post, leading one of the Coalborough schools in challenging circumstances. The newly appointed headteacher was seen to be less transformational in her approach than the longer-serving headteachers. However, even the more experienced headteachers provided evidence that their level of transformational leadership had increased since leading their current school, even if they had previously served as headteachers in other schools. Such evidence could suggest that it is leading a school within an area of high social deprivation that had, in some part, encouraged these headteachers to become more transformational, with a stronger focus on developing individuals and expanding their horizons and potential.

The development of transformational leadership characteristics may also have been influenced by the leader's core values and their desire to see fairness and equality for all. When serving in a socially deprived area, there is a belief that students are not exposed to the same opportunities or life chances that others receive, and as such there is a desire to provide more for them, especially in developing the way they see the world and raising their aspirations. Another common theme that emerged from these interviews was the feeling on the part of these headteachers that it was a privilege to serve a socially deprived area. They were all convinced that they were able to make a significant contribution to the community in which their school was situated, and believed they had made significant improvements to the life chances and aspirations of students within their schools. These convictions would lead to the beliefs being manifested in actions. It is possible that a community that is socially deprived has more scope for the actions taken by headteachers to have a bigger impact and therefore yields greater results and greater rewards for the headteachers. This in turn would encourage the headteachers to become even more transformational and to seek more opportunities to transform the lives of those within their schools.

5

Deploying Transformational Leadership: Strategies for Challenging Circumstances

The aim of the original research study of leadership of four schools in challenging circumstances was to explore the extent to which transactional and transformational leadership were deployed by headteachers in each of the participating schools in the socially deprived local authority of Coalborough. The resultant data have already been analysed in Chapters 3 and 4. These chapters illustrated where each of the leadership styles was used in each of the participating schools. It is now possible to determine how far transactional leadership was used and to identify the strategies that enabled headteachers successfully to deploy transformational leadership. This chapter begins with an analysis of how heads deploy transformational leadership and then examines how far they consider themselves to be transformational. It goes on to explore the key features of transformational leadership in schools to ascertain how far heads recognized the importance of values, building relationships, handling unpredictability and motivating staff. In so doing the strategies used by these headteachers in schools in challenging circumstances are established. The chapter concludes by examining the evidence that is available to estimate how far such strategies have been successful in these schools. In part, the success of such strategies depends on how far headteachers in these schools intentionally committed themselves to the deployment of transformational leadership. Such intentionality is central to the success of all school leaders.

The deployment of transformational leadership

A key feature of transformational school leaders is the ability intentionally to make lasting and profound changes to the view of the world and underpinning values held by some pupils, staff and members of the wider community. The headteachers in this study considered this ability to be essential for serving in these socially deprived schools, an approach that was articulated by the head of Yarborough School when he described how he felt he needed to change the culture of the entire community, so that the community members valued education more:

> We currently have generations of parents who had pretty poor experiences in our school and *de facto* that's instilled upon their siblings about the value of their schools and I think that's probably the factor of all schools in the areas where the socio-economic conditions are less favourable. So, there's a significant job to do there in changing the culture of communities as well and I believe that through learning that can be achieved.

The same head then proceeded to detail his opinion that the values and beliefs of the school needed to be embedded in others in order to improve the perception they have of themselves:

> I think professional development and continuing professional development for all staff including associate staff and anybody who works in the organization whether it's the dinner ladies, the cleaners, you know, they've all got to be involved in the shared values and beliefs in the organization about, and that's about developing respect, self-respect, self-esteem, self-worth.

His belief, therefore, is that what is needed to improve a school in a challenging socially deprived area is a change in self-belief. This headteacher felt that his responsibility was to deal with this to affect the entire community's level of deprivation:

> 38% of our students have lone parents, 51% live in the poorest 10% of housing stock in the country and 21% on free meals and indices of multiple deprivation are high and I think those issues we've got to tackle, the issue to do with child poverty.

The way he was achieving this, he concluded, was by 'bringing about a cultural change'.

The belief that he needed to bring about a change in the perceptions of others, both inside and outside the school, was also a key priority for the headteacher of Greville School, and one that was not limited to members of the school:

[We] have worked very hard on looking at changes in culture and belief . . . I think probably the more time you spend in the teaching profession, the more you see it as a way to bring about change, and benefit to people's lives, both young people and again I think in addition to that the wider community as well, and the impact that you can have is immeasurable isn't it, in how you can change people's lives for the better and improve society.

The constructivist paradigm (Lambert, 2009) would suggest that this belief – that the headteacher should and can make a major change – would direct his actions towards implementing it and would result in the change being manifested. This has proved to be the case.

The newly appointed headteacher of Blackwood School had a different view. She noted the changes that needed to take place and also the extent of these changes, but set about bringing about those changes through transactional rather than transformational leadership, since she focused more on tasks than on people. She described how her vision would require new procedures, saying that the school needed a 'real radical change in terms of following procedures, so a real willingness to recognize that changes have to be made in a short space of time, and actually getting on and doing it'.

This contrasted with the transformational style of the headteacher of Greville School, who talked about his school priority, stating that 'the vision is really to ensure that we raise aspirations', a vision that had become part of the school ethos. The deputy of this school expressed a similar approach when she explained that the vision was all about 'raising aspiration and achievement and it's the aspiration comes first and I think the achievement follows that'. She also explained how this was achieved by altering the self-belief of students: '[We] give them some belief in themselves. So I think in terms of raising aspiration, raising achievement that is, it is the vision of the school.'

The creation of a shared vision is not only a feature of transformational leadership but also one that headteachers in these schools considered to be mandatory. Furthermore, as Southworth (1998) describes, the transformational leader ensures that the vision is carried by others and is at the heart of their actions. This was evident when the deputy of Yarborough School explained how the school vision was being implemented:

So I'd say that it's the leadership team...who now start to drive that vision, not just one individual person...we did a visioning day with all the staff as part of the training day and we asked them to look out what would be their vision for the college and the community.

The involvement of stakeholders in the creation of the vision gives them some ownership of the vision. This was also noted by the headteacher of Greville School, who described how the vision was generated by

all staff really and it's not just staff, it's been the whole community really both parents, students, governors, partners of the school, have all been involved in creating that vision...the engagement of the community is paramount to me and the way that we communicate that is by involving them really.

Transformational leaders involve others in the creation of the vision as a means of motivating them to act on it, a point noted by the head of Yarborough School when he explained how he involved others in the creation of the vision, but still used this as a means of altering the perceptions of those involved:

Staff are very much involved in the vision. I think the vision has to emanate from the leadership, the leader of the school and it comes I think from their own personal beliefs and values, but if it's not something that is shared, then people don't buy into it and I think in that respect, there's a lot of perhaps coaxing, mentoring and a lot of work to be done in sharing and agreeing the values of visions.

A similar stance was taken by the headteacher of Greville School when he explained how he considered everyone to be a leader, from the cleaners to kitchen staff and from the students to heads of department. He expressed his view that the involvement of others was needed to bring about change, because 'that's the best way in my opinion, in the circumstances that our school is in, that you can bring about change and effect change'. This does not mean that the headteachers were manipulating people to achieve their own gains. Rather, they believed that they were acting in the best interests of their followers. This belief was articulated by the headteacher of Yarborough School, who said: 'I would describe myself as being passionate about people, without necessarily agreeing with them all the time and of course also having to do some difficult things with people which does affect their lives.' He proceeded to explain that his motivation was to empower others to succeed; this also is one of the underpinning features of transactional leadership.

It is evident that all the headteachers in this first part of this study referred to the need to alter the self-image of their followers. This was seen as a way to raise aspirations and to enable others to share in the vision of an alternative, better future for all. The data revealed a theme amongst headteachers, in that they involve others in the creation of a vision, inspiring them to believe in the vision as a real way forward. This involvement was not restricted to members of the school but also extended to members of the community, revealing that headteachers were aware of the importance of altering the perceptions of all members of a community living within a socially deprived area. This demonstrates the extent to which transformational leadership is significant in schools in challenging circumstances, as revealed by the importance these headteachers placed on the inclusion of values, the creation of a vision and the involvement of others. The headteachers felt that the way to regenerate a community and break the cycle of families being born into and remaining in poverty was not only by improving the achievements of their students but also by transforming the perceptions of the students and the community in which they live.

Headteachers' perceptions of themselves as transformational leaders

Once it is accepted that headteachers in this study, who were serving in schools facing challenging circumstances, accredited some of their success to the ability to behave as transformational leaders by attempting to alter the perceptions of others, the question of to what extent they regarded themselves as transformational leaders and, as such, constructed a reality in which they were transformational arises. The deputy of Raleigh School expressed a desire for the leadership to become more transformational: 'I would say it's getting there. Yes. I think…hand on heart I couldn't say it's totally there, I think it is getting there.' Nevertheless, the headteachers and deputies in this study stated that they believed that their leadership was to some extent transformational. As the head of Yarborough School put it: 'I think transformation of schools is something evidentially that I've been able to achieve.' Furthermore, their success could be attributed to the deployment of transformational leadership:

> I think [school leadership] is transformational, you only need to look at where the school was and where it is now, and the way that we operate and the way that we work and the way that we manage relationships.

The recognition of this ability to make significant changes and the focus of headteachers, described earlier, on altering the aspirations and self-belief of people provide evidence that these headteachers were intentionally acting as transformational leaders, both for individuals and for wider communities. This is especially important for schools in challenging circumstances where the headteachers believe that the entire community needs to be empowered, to allow them to believe in a future vision where they can help themselves and achieve. One possible benefit of serving in a deprived area is that the actions taken by headteachers have a proportionately greater impact on the lives of children and the general community, due to some community members having less access to enriching experiences. In order to succeed, headteachers in these areas need to maintain levels of optimism that prevent them from being negatively affected by the depressing and potentially demotivating surroundings. The modelling of this positivity is a characteristic noticed by Kurland *et al.* (2010) and is evident in vision-focused, transformational leaders. The level of deprivation within the communities where these schools are situated may create a situation where there is greater feedback to headteachers, as they can easily see the benefits of their actions, encouraging them to develop their level of transformational leadership to a greater extent than if they served in a different school. Indeed all the headteachers in this study viewed themselves as transformational in their operations, with an awareness of how they had shaped communities, transformed the lives of others and altered the self-belief of socially deprived individuals through their creation of a positive vision and the communication of this vision with as many stakeholders as possible.

Vision and communication in transformational leadership

Kurland *et al.* (2010) found that being vision-focused is a common trait of transformational leaders and one that is needed to successfully deploy leadership in a transformational manner. In a school in an area with a high degree of social deprivation this is even more important, as most of the heads of these schools felt that they need to create a vision that not only affects the school but also infiltrates the beliefs of the entire community, as revealed by the deputy of Greville School: 'These children come from very deprived environments themselves. I think for me it's about making a difference to that community it's about trying to engage with people.'

Not all the heads subscribed to the view that wide participation in creating the vision for the school was essential. The newly appointed head of Blackwood School discussed aspects of creating a vision when she explained that it has to be 'top down, because of the very nature of people I suppose coming in at senior leadership team level and saying this is how we are going to do things now'. In this instance, this headteacher demonstrated a lack of transformational leadership attitudes regarding the involvement of others, which was very different from the approach described earlier by the headteachers of Greville and Yarborough schools.

Nevertheless, the majority view among the headteachers in this study was that engaging members of the wider school community in the creation of the vision was important. The vehicle for this was the process of communicating an inspiring vision where people see themselves as capable of changing. The Greville School headteacher explained how he communicated the vision effectively by involving people in it: 'The greatest way to communicate is to involve people isn't it…that's what we've done.' He described how he wrote to parents and invited them to attend a visioning session where they could play a part in the creation of the school vision. He expressed the importance of this:

> I think if people have bought into your vision and feel that they've been included in that then they're going to shift and they're going to move towards that end point, whatever that end point is because there never is one, you know but it's that continuing to improve. I think that if people feel that they've been invested in and that they've been listened to and that they've been supported and been given their opportunity that they will move along with you.

This belief that the way to effectively implement a vision in a community of high social deprivation is to involve others in its creation becomes manifest, as it influences future actions. To be truly transformed people must first alter their mindset to focus on positivity, which will in turn empower them to act upon this belief, enabling the creation of a new, more positive future. A similar form of transformation was expressed by the Yarborough School headteacher, who explained how he communicated the vision by ensuring that he was consistently on message, both in all his conversations and in his actions. This level of consistency plays a major role in the transformation of others and was also underlined by the head of Blackwood School who took a similar position, maintaining that the message needed to be carried consistently by everyone, not only the headteacher: 'We are about creating culture and ethos and mission, mission statement, call it what you will, vision that everybody's singing from the same hymn sheet.' She also pointed out that a failure to achieve this would result in the vision not being achieved, because the transformation of ethos would not occur:

> It has to be an ethos in its true way because ultimately it is what's going on behind every classroom door and if we as leaders don't really encourage every member of staff to share that vision it's not going to happen.

Communication can be seen, therefore, to be an essential part of achieving the vision in order to transform followers.

There is little doubt that the headteachers in this study were guided by a vision of a better future, which is a prerequisite for transformational leadership. In an area of high social deprivation families may not value education highly, and often do not see it as a means of breaking out of the poverty in which they find themselves, believing that schools have very little to do with the lives of people within the community (Harris, 2002). The headteachers in these challenging circumstances used vision and communication to transform the perceptions of others, revealing new ways of thinking and behaving that empowered pupils, parents and members of the wider community to take action to help themselves. The level of communication required to share the vision effectively, so that it is carried through the entire community, was dependent on the ability of these headteachers to influence followers and build strong relationships with stakeholders.

Valuing and building relationships

Harris (2003) noted how headteachers who were successful transformational leaders fostered strong relationships between all parties who worked in their school. This is also evident from the data from the main study where headteachers all expressed the view that relationships should be based on mutual respect; as the headteacher of Blackwood School stated, a 'belief in mutual respect…informs everything I do'. The headteacher of Yarborough School described how respect too was essential to engage students:

> It's a relationship which is engaging and I talk a lot about the culture of compelling engagement and what that means. I think essentially it's about two-way respect and that is about self-respect and it's about being approachable and it is being prepared to listen to people and not always agreeing with them. I think that's one of the biggest challenges that faces the school and there is no doubt and we can agree or disagree with it but you know, the school, the success of schools is about people who lead them from the top in terms of the impact that they have and then how students identify with them.

Headteachers, therefore, attach great importance to relationships in a school with a high level of social deprivation. The headteacher of Greville School also noted that, in his opinion, it is the challenging circumstances of the school that require this emphasis on relationships, stating that relationships were critical, 'in a school like mine anyway'. This headteacher recalled how he had focused on building a strong relationship between the school and the community from the very start:

> Within about two days I was down in the community talking to parents, often about issues with students, but actually in the community talking to parents and trying to find solutions, so building relationships right at that point.

The headteachers discussed the importance of building partnerships between parents, the school and the community, with the headteacher of Blackwood School stating that she felt privileged to be able to serve a deprived area and form relationships, as she believed the key to improving education in such areas is in the three-way partnership between the school, the students and the community. This illustrates the level of value headteachers placed on the relationships that formed within schools, and the actions they took to facilitate those productive relationships in order to contribute to the development of the school. Through this belief, headteachers constructed strong relationships that provided transformational leaders with the ability to transform the perceptions of others, allowing a level of fluidity where thoughts and beliefs can be adapted to meet the changing needs of schools. Communities of high social deprivation are influenced greatly by political decisions and levels of recession; national trends can have a dramatic impact on the number of people in a family who have work, and on the financial benefits they receive. If headteachers are to influence communities of high deprivation, they need to be able to change quickly to meet the changing circumstances in which their communities find themselves.

Handling unpredictability

A significant feature of transformational leaders is that their belief in people provides them with an inner confidence that enables them to allow their organization to evolve, instead of having to restrict everything to make it fit a predesigned template. Harris (2003) confirms that this is a key feature of transformational leaders and one that reveals that transformational behaviour is taking place. The headteachers demonstrated different methods of handling unpredictability. The Blackwood School head described how she held onto the underpinning vision and refused to allow circumstances to deviate her from this vision:

> I don't think I will ever deviate from that vision, because otherwise it's not worth the paper it's written on, is it? The methods by which I achieve that vision, the deadlines, the timings may have to change, so I'm not to get

frustrated and impatient with people, I need to recognize that sometimes practical situations may mean that it can't happen then, or that particular thing can't happen, so I might have to just adapt it, and compromises may have to be made along the way, but students will always come first in that compromise decision, priorities may have to change, but I've got to keep, I've got to keep the vision, because otherwise it will all just crumble won't it.

The headteacher of Greville School agreed, noting the importance of generating enough momentum to carry changes forward through unpredicted circumstances. This was achieved in his school:

> By being distributive I think and look[ing] at things in a way that tends to minimize issues. Where they do arise I suppose then you challenge that don't you, and you know, I think staff in the school and kids and parents are aware of where [Greville] is going, and what we want to achieve and what we want to do and people buy into that.

The headteacher of Raleigh School described how he continually reassesses the situation and identifies what aspects can be salvaged and what changes need to be made:

> If it's blocked, or we can't do it, that has to be annoying first, because otherwise we wouldn't have wanted to do it. If we haven't thought it through to a point where we think it is right and . . . sustainable . . . we shouldn't have actually been doing it. So if it blocks it, we've lost something from the original concept haven't we. OK, go around again; what could we salvage out of that? . . . the trouble is you can't always salvage an idea, if you can do half of it, it may be better not to do any of it, because it actually was a whole package . . . But on the other hand, usually out of that emerges a way forward which says OK if we are not doing this, or we have to do it that way for very, very powerful reasons, can we get back to that?

In order to drive his school forward, the headteacher of Yarborough School incorporated change management into his daily practices and imparted this not only to his team but to everyone in his school. This was based on being a critical thinker:

> We've got to be very much reviewers in our lives and we've also got to be strategic thinkers and very objective thinkers and I think one of the things which is critical in terms of what we do is how we handle situations and so what stops you in your track and because I think that's an appropriate issue.

This head felt change management was a necessary part of school improvement, and should be something that everyone was trained for and expected. It is evident that the sets of data from each of the schools provided instances where the headteachers of those schools acted as transformational leaders, and it is possible that their main areas of school success could be explained by the extent to which headteachers view themselves as successful leaders who are able to lead in times of change by motivating and inspiring others.

All the headteachers identified different methods of dealing with change and unpredictability. Although it is difficult to rank the individual responses, it could be argued that the headteachers of Yarborough and Raleigh schools were transformational in their approach due to their expectation of the need to reflect and adapt. Similarly, the headteacher of Greville School, by utilizing the diverse skills of others to form a team that had the ability to handle unexpected situations, could also be viewed as transformational. However, the headteacher of Blackwood School used a fixed vision and was unwilling to deviate from it; such an approach could be transformational in its use of a vision, but could also be seen as transactional in its reluctance to adapt or change.

The use of motivation as a vehicle for achievement

Schools situated in areas of high deprivation are faced with students who have low aspirations and a lack of self-belief. The headteachers in this study noted that it was essential to change this ethos if the school was going to improve. A key aspect of transformational leaders is that they lead through motivation (Hartog, 2003). The belief that the development of people is the motivating force that leads them to achieve was expressed by the headteacher of Yarborough School, who shared his thoughts on training young people to become change managers. In a school faced with challenging circumstances, this head's focus was on raising the aspirations and the self-belief of an entire community. Empowering students to become change managers in the community could accelerate the improvement and create a level of sustainability where the community members become actively involved in bringing about changes. He explained that 'my vision always is being focused on young people first and foremost and how we can enable and empower them to become successful adults and how they can become the change managers'.

If headteachers are to deploy transformational leadership successfully, their colleagues must carry the message with motivation and inspiration and the headteachers must believe in this as a vehicle for achievement, in order to construct it. When members of a school in challenging circumstances are motivated, they develop a belief in themselves that alters their actions, enabling them to overcome the mental barriers associated with poverty. The head of Raleigh School highlighted this when he used the metaphor of motivated students going through walls:

> When they're not motivated you will not move one millimetre, they'll be very nice about it, they don't get in your face, they just won't do it, it won't get done. Motivated, they'll go through walls, they go through walls every week, that's the beauty of being here.

The positive emotions that this requires in all parties are generated, according to Cameron (2006), when people experience virtuousness and value-based leadership, which elevates them to new levels of job satisfaction and pride, motivating them to achieve more. This is in agreement with the findings of Sun (2009) who states that transformational leaders empower colleagues to 'realize the organizational goals and even make extra efforts for the benefit of the organization' (Cameron, 2006: 352).

Relaying personal values in communications

It is widely accepted (Bell and Stevenson, 2006; Hartog, 2003) that for transformational leadership to be deployed successfully, leaders must relay their values through the interactions they have with others. This is particularly important in schools in challenging circumstances, due to the level of motivation and personal pride that can be generated through value-based leadership (Cameron, 2006). The data collected from the headteachers in this study illustrated clearly the importance they attached to relaying their own values in their communications. When considering the significance of transformational leadership in schools in challenging circumstances, it became evident that the headteachers had a belief that students in socially deprived areas deserve more. All the heads in this study believed that social and economic deprivation needed to be tackled, and this belief shaped the ways in which they approached what they did:

> Our community here is in I think, one of the most deprived constituencies in terms of, you know, the basic sort of income of our young people, or our families. If that's the case, and I do believe...[it is, then] the way that you affect a person's life chances is by the qualifications that they receive and therefore the number of paths that are open for them to choose what they want to do.

A similar desire was reported by the headteacher of Blackwood School who described how all parents have aspirations and want the best for their children: 'it's not just a middle-class...aspiration that their children do well, I don't believe that. I think it is something inbuilt in any parent'.

The headteacher of Greville School outlined a way of tackling one of the key problems facing schools in challenging circumstances, that of the disruptive behaviour of pupils, describing how he related to the worst-behaved children in his school: 'even the students who present challenging behaviour sometimes, when you are talking to them individually, then you know, you can get through to them'. This headteacher also stated directly that he looked for the best in people: 'I am a very positive person and I always look for the best in people and in situations and I think that's the only way that you should live your life really.' This attitude was demonstrated most clearly by the headteacher of Yarborough School who confirmed his faith in the aspiration of the whole community, including those families in economic and social poverty. It was also clear that he believed in the school's role as an enabler of positive change in that community:

> I would describe the community around our school as mixed and I think it ranges from middle-class, fairly successful, aspirational and affluent to poverty you know, and not just economic poverty but social poverty as well in terms of families, in terms of their aspiration and in terms of their expectations and yet, what I also see in every bit of our community is hope. I do believe that the vast majority of people don't want to be trapped inside with some of the negativity which they portray but they just don't know how they're going to get out of where they are.

This evidence shows a belief that people retain an element of hope and would like to break free from the negative habits and negative circumstances in which they find themselves. It also reveals the extent to which this head, at least, saw the school and its leadership as having a key role to play in the wider, socially deprived community. It could be argued that the headteachers' beliefs and attitudes manifest a reality where the children within the school are motivated by the headteacher to become aspirational in their own views.

The headteacher of Blackwood School also revealed a desire to make fundamental changes to the daily behaviour of people:

> I don't just mean teaching staff, it is about an ethos and a culture. It is about respect and the way we all treat each other and speak to each other, it's every member of staff who works in our institution.

Heads from all the schools in Coalborough made references to the need to teach better behaviour, with the headteacher of Greville School referring to the behaviour of some students as 'challenging' and the head of Raleigh School describing how he had one-to-one chats with students to modify their behaviour. The manner in which people relate to each other was also mentioned by the head of Yarborough School, who expressed his belief that 'a lot of our schools have got to become kinder places in terms of, you know, how we speak to each other and what our expectations are'.

Another strong underpinning belief shared by the headteachers was the desire for everyone to achieve and do well, particularly against a background of challenging circumstances:

> I just think there is so much potential, in this school, so my vision is about realizing the potential of every child in this school.

This deep-rooted belief in better opportunities for children in a socially deprived area is an example of what Davies and Brighouse (2010) term 'passionate leadership with a moral foundation'. The headteachers shared their values and vision but went beyond this to construct an environment where people learned from each other, so that everyone was developed. This goes beyond a duty to achieve for students when attending the school to a broader desire to achieve, both for students after they leave and for other members of the community. The desire of these headteachers to go beyond their school responsibilities and affect the lives of the community is a choice that reflects their purpose and their wish to improve the lives of others, where they perceive there to be a lack due to high levels of poverty and social challenge.

This purpose was reflected by the headteacher of Yarborough School who spoke of the 'learning journey' of young people:

> I often say that I'm on a mission and I often say I am doing missionary work, and I think being a headteacher is a privilege. I think to shape people's lives, to shape the learning journey of young people, to shape the learning journey of the school and to develop the community are very privileged things to be able to do. I think if you've got the skills to do it, it's a great gift and you know, I feel fortunate that I can do it and I think demonstratively so.

These statements not only provide an insight into each headteacher's personal values but also offer an understanding of their viewpoints and underpinning belief in helping people. The links between transformational leadership and the character and values of the leader are addressed by Bass and Steidlmeier (2006) who argue that one is characterized by the other, and they cannot be separated. The values that these headteachers carried with them may be responsible for their desire to work in a socially deprived area where they perceive they can make a bigger difference. The headteachers believed in people; they believed in raising aspirations where they were low; and they believed in providing opportunities for all. Such beliefs allow the conviction that it is possible to transform the lives of others, a belief which can also be understood in terms of transformational leadership, which facilitates the changes to people's lives that the headteachers hope to achieve. This then provides the headteachers with evidence that their actions are successful, which in turn spurs them to become more action-driven, transforming the lives of even more people; this could explain why transformational leadership is more successful in schools in challenging circumstances.

Headteachers as transformational leaders: The evidence for success

When headteachers are transformational, they create a workforce of staff who share the school's vision, share model organizational values and demonstrate high performance (Bush, 2003). They are involved in the decision-making processes and their levels of creativity are fostered to form an organization that is focused on the development of people, while being able to adapt to unexpected changes in order to maintain improvement. It is these features that led the headteachers in this study to consider transformational leadership to be linked very strongly to their areas of success. In this particular study, the ability to raise the aspirations and self-belief of others, while simultaneously being able to adapt quickly to political changes, was very important for the success of schools in challenging circumstances. When attempting to measure the level of this success a range of criteria were available: some tangible, such as examination results, and some less tangible, such as changes in ethos. Any analysis of the data in order to seek evidence of successful leadership in these schools must focus, therefore, on the impact that these headteachers believed they have had: the impact on students' achievement; the impact on raising their aspirations; the impact on relationships within the school; the impact on staff and student motivation; the changes in status for the schools; and finally, the impact these headteachers have had on the wider community.

Impact on students

There is clear evidence that the headteachers had a positive impact on both the aspirations and achievements of students within their schools. Aspiration and achievement are thought to be linked, as the headteacher of Greville

School highlighted when he stated his belief that his achievements could be accredited to the changes he had secured in altering the students' self-belief:

> Ten years ago our students really didn't believe in themselves; they didn't believe they could do it and so there was a change in ethos that went off and it started with the staff, but it is about a change in belief that went on in getting our students to think and believe that they could also do it.

This improvement is evident in Greville School's achievement of a high Contextual Value-Added score (see Appendix 1), revealing that students attending this school made more progress than most other schools in similar circumstances. This improvement also applied to less tangible areas, such as the shift that the school has made in the attitudes and aspirations of students. The Greville School headteacher explained how the school had effected this to such an extent that 'when students do come to us, they soon become engaged in their work. They want to learn and they want to achieve and they want to aspire to better things.' He described how he believed they had transformed followers by changing the way students view themselves, and detailed how the vision has encompassed this, since 'the vision is really to ensure that we raise aspirations and we raise achievement for all young people'. He also pointed out that every child who left the school at the end of the previous year either continued with their education or secured employment, a statistic of which he was proud.

The headteacher at Raleigh School was also concerned about raising the aspirations of students. Part of his strategy was to ensure that students 'contribute by doing, I sometimes don't necessarily communicate first go, and I know that, or second go, or third go, but we keep communicating'. This approach was also demonstrated by the deputy of Greville School, who explained that it has taken a great deal of time to achieve the success they have had, and that they had managed to raise aspirations and achievement by creating a vision that was now shared throughout the school and was understood by the majority of people within it. She underlined the impact that the sharing of a vision can have on raising the aspirations of children from a community with a high level of social deprivation. This approach was based not only on improving examination results but also on providing an extremely wide range of pastoral activities that are designed to extend the boundaries of the students beyond their immediate location:

> One of the big things that we have done also is as well as the exam results we try and get the kids an absolutely massive range of pastoral activities, we do trips all over the place, there's hundreds of them go, they are going to Canada this year. But, just about, there are the large trips but just about giving them the opportunity to look a little bit further than [this town] and

to raise their aspiration, and realize there is a big world out there and that it is not just centred around [villages within this town] and I think that is how our aim our goal and to give these kids the best chance in life that we can.

Greville School also demonstrated instances of success that could be attributed to aspects of transformational leadership. For example, it was important to the headteacher that students in this community were developed as whole people, by not focusing solely on exam results. It is important, therefore, 'to ensure that students do not only leave school with good qualifications but also as good citizens'.

Throughout the interviews the headteachers referred to the need to raise the aspirations and the self-belief of learners, as they felt this was essential in a school in challenging circumstances. The headteachers from all schools described their greatest change as their change in ethos; as the Yarborough School head observed: 'I think the biggest change [at this school] has been cultural change.' The headteachers believed that their ability to raise aspirations was as important as anything else they were able to achieve, and it was a result of their ability to form and foster strong relationships.

Impact on relationships

The relationships headteachers wanted to foster throughout the school were modelled by the headteachers themselves. As the deputy of Raleigh School put it: 'you get to the working relationship, so I feel that that's very much led by the head's own working relationships with us'. These school leaders felt that their relationships were part of their transformational leadership style and were in part responsible for the outcomes they achieved. For example, when describing the leadership of his school, the headteacher of Greville School said:

> I think it is transformational, you only need to look at where the school was and where it is now and the way that we operate and the way that we work in managing relationships and situations has led to a massive increase in outcomes and long may it continue.

He also stressed his understanding that relationships are essential for the success of a school in challenging circumstances. This headteacher's belief that cultures need changing to generate improvement relies upon the ability to form strong relationships across all parties:

> If you're going to talk about change and improvement I think that for me one of the absolutely key things that's led to that change and that shift in

culture and dynamic is relationships across the board. I think relationships between staff and students, relationships amongst staff, relationships with parents, all of these things are absolutely critical really in terms of improvement, in my opinion, in a school like mine anyway.

He then quoted the statistics of the school's most recent student questionnaire, which showed that 98 percent of students expressed the opinion that Greville School was a good place to be.

It was also evident that headteachers valued not only their own professional relationships but also those throughout the school. For example, the Greville School headteacher described his pride when staff run pastoral trips for students: 'the staff are prepared to put on [a range of trips] for students again [which] builds those very positive relationships and that I would say is intrinsic really to improvement'. The deputy headteachers also shared first-hand experience of the value that headteachers place upon positive relationships, as all felt they had a very strong, positive relationship with their headteacher. The deputy of Blackwood School described his relationship with the head as:

an open relationship and it's about and what [the Head] has done in that she has been completely honest and forthright and hidden nothing from me and it's about that ownership that I feel that I've got ownership within the leadership of the College and again that I know that I can trust [the Head], I can talk to [her] about anything, you know, let's say there are particularly difficulties without actually feeling intimidated I'm not feeling the fact that you know I've failed by asking...it's a very constructive relationship.

He also described the headteacher as being 'extremely supportive'. A similar message was relayed by the deputy of Raleigh School, who described her relationship with the headteacher as being:

very positive, very warm, there is a lot of mutual respect and trust there, I certainly feel that, I certainly feel that I am trusted to take the initiative and get on and crack on with things that I don't necessarily need to bother him with all the time although I am conscious to make sure that he's in agreement with the decisions that I'm making.

The same deputy also revealed that she thinks the headteacher has selected staff because of the relationships he knows he can form with them. She expressed a view that she and the other deputy headteachers share the belief that they were selected for their differences and the contribution their diversity can bring to the school:

Myself and another colleague were appointed at the same time to do specific things at that time and we often say that [the Head] obviously had a very clear idea in his head what he wanted. We work well together, we complement each other but we are totally different and whether by accident or design that has benefited both of us and we believe the school. I'm sure there's been an element of planned approach to the recruitment of certain members of the leadership team.

The headteachers felt that positive relationships were essential to the success of their schools, with the headteacher of Greville School stating that focusing on relationships was 'absolutely key' to motivating followers.

Impact on staff and student motivation

The interviews revealed that headteachers believed in motivation as a vehicle for achievement. They describe their staff as motivated which, when examined through the constructivist paradigm, would manifest in the way the headteacher communicates and relates to staff, encouraging them to become the way they are represented in the headteacher's thoughts. The headteacher of Greville School pointed out:

We are a highly motivated staff, I think and I include myself in that as well and again I think that's because we work very closely and collectively as a team. It's evident throughout the whole of the school really, there's lots of professional dialogue that goes on lots of thinking about learning and pedagogy, people feel that we are a school that is moving forward, that's prepared to take risks, that they won't be discouraged from taking risks and it's positively encouraged really. So we're always looking to innovate and to learn best practice or next practice from other schools, from other colleagues.

The Yarborough School deputy also described the Senior Leadership Team as motivated. He went on to describe how this could be credited to the headteacher:

In eight years [the Head] has put together a team of individuals who are all happy in their positions, who are all motivated in their positions...there is not one person around that table that I am not confident that they can do their job and I think that's the key aspect of [the Head's] leadership and what he's left is that legacy, he's left that ability for us to continue to evolve and develop as a college because we have got the individuals who can do that and it is about taking risks on some people.

The headteacher of Raleigh School pointed out the benefits of having people who are motivated. As quoted earlier in this chapter, he explained how people can 'go through walls' when the level of motivation is right. He went on to describe how motivated staff become 'a hell of a power house'. This is a particular advantage in a school in challenging circumstances where staff members need to overcome the apathy and low self-esteem associated with poverty and deprivation. He also described how he motivated people by praising them wherever possible, no matter how small the achievement. He believed that you should always use praise, as this can inspire people. Although other headteachers did not explicitly draw attention to this fact, it should be noted that all four of the deputy headteachers viewed themselves as motivated, which could be the result of working alongside a transformational leader.

The headteachers also noted how the involvement and development of staff could lead to colleagues becoming more personally motivated and hence result in greater achievement. The head of Greville School explained that

> engaging the community, different stakeholders, that's part of their development as well and I think that if you're involving staff comprehensively then in your way you are trying to reach a vision and you're trying to lead a school into a particular direction. That in itself is developmental.

The deputy headteacher of this school pointed out that the head was a great believer in providing opportunities for staff to develop themselves. She attributed her own career progression within the school to this, as well as her loyalty to that school. She explained how, when she was Head of Science, she was encouraged to take the National Professional Qualification for Headteachers (NPQH). She acknowledged:

> We probably, for a small school, have the highest percentage of staff that hold the NPQH. Probably more than most of the schools in the country because [the Head] is always the one to say you know you can do this.

The headteacher of Yarborough School also set out to develop people at all levels, to affect their self-image by fostering 'shared values and beliefs in the organization'. His deputy provided evidence of how this headteacher's honest approach instilled his staff with confidence: 'He's always been honest with me and...I've always been confident and comfortable in my position in school and he's instilled that in me.' This head's transformational leadership style could also be seen in the impact that he had made on the Senior Leadership Team. As the deputy head noted, not only had the head created a leadership team who were all motivated and happy in their positions, but more importantly he 'left that ability for us to continue to evolve and develop as a college because we have got the individuals who can do that and it is about taking risks on some people'. This approach to staff development at Yarborough School was based on the extent to which the head was 'good at spotting potential, putting you in place and letting you make mistakes but then supporting you in those mistakes as well'. The headteacher, therefore, was able to motivate and inspire his team to the extent that they felt empowered and driven to create improvements. In a school in challenging circumstances, the development of more transformational leaders at all levels of the school provides a greater ability to adapt more quickly.

Conversely, the strong belief that headteachers had in motivation as a vehicle for success was also demonstrated in a negative form by the head of Blackwood School when she expressed her opinion about staff who were not motivated. She pointed out that:

> the majority [of staff are] very motivated, having said that, even in the short time I've been here I am aware that for some staff, they are not on the bus and I can see that already, they haven't got that amount of passion and drive and motivation about putting young people first, that is my vision, and ultimately people make a decision and I think for the majority that would be a positive decision, but maybe not for all.

This could be linked to the newly appointed headteacher's current emphasis on transactional leadership rather than transformational, resulting in only partial success in motivating staff.

Changes to the status of the school

The change of status involved in schools becoming Specialist Colleges may also have a motivating effect on staff and students. The headteacher of Raleigh School described how he had successfully gained engineering status which, he stated, was an indicator of high performance:

> What we've changed is that we've taken, I hope, everything that made the previous [Raleigh School] successful and we've interpreted it very differently, two specialisms, high-performing specialist schools status, engineering.... and applied learning has been the obvious one to come after that. The concept that this school would be able to achieve National Status for applied learning six years ago, vocational applied learning, no it would have been not accepted, it's just taken as blindingly obvious now, that that's where we go next.

All the headteachers were proud of their Specialist Status. It was seen as an achievement and was offered by the deputy headteacher of Greville School as evidence of school improvement, and led to the further achievement of becoming a mentor for other schools. She detailed how the school

> has become a trust school. We became an RATL school which is a Raising Attainment Transforming Learning school for the SSAT [Specialist Schools and Academies Trust] and we're an accredited mentor school with them. So in terms of titles they're the changes that occurred but within that obviously there are so many things that change within the school at the same time when becoming a specialist technology college. Changes in terms of student outcome, we've come from – in 2000 we were 15%, 5 plus A*s to C. This year we were at 74%, for last set of results.

Although the change from school to Specialist College is only a structural change, it does reward the schools with additional community funding, enabling them to become more involved with the community.

Impact on the wider community

All the schools which took part in the first part of this study were community schools, and the headteachers viewed their community involvement as a very important measure of their success. The headteacher of Yarborough described himself as a key player in the transformation of the community. He later went on to say:

> School leaders have a pre-eminent role in terms of shaping the future of communities and that they have to be seen in some of the public debates about the regeneration issues and about the future of what's going on.

This headteacher took every opportunity to promote this vision at community events, and had spoken at the local church. His deputy at this school reinforced this, saying that the head was constantly communicating with community groups, including addressing the town council. A similar intention to effect positive change in the community was demonstrated by the head of Greville School, who expressed the idea that his school was an engine for change:

> My impact or the school's impact, it's not for me to say, but I think that it has been crucial and I think it will continue to be significant as well because of some of the things that we are proposing to put in place around our

cooperative trust, on co-location of services onto school site, so really the school, even though we are outside of the community, will be at the very heart of the community, and be really an engine for change I think, an engine for improvement in the broader community.

This understanding of the transformational potential of headteachers throughout the community was shared by the head of Blackwood School:

We're affecting what happens to this community, because if the young people here have a pride and an attachment to their community and yet they go on and do wonderful things with their lives, or maybe you know, stay on in the sixth form for example, to be the first to do that in the family and then the next step, be the first to go on to higher education, it's going to take time and a couple of generations to make that difference but it will make the difference to what's going on around here.

She also pointed out: 'That's recognizing I suppose that headteachers or leaders in education have a great deal of influence and power and actually I suppose they do.'

This acceptance that schools have an influence on their community was of concern to the head of Yarborough School, who felt that schools needed to change the attitudes of people, even if they were disenfranchised:

I think schools, if they are to become the heart of the communities, have the key role to play in challenging and changing the culture of communities and improving the aspiration, attitudes and values of the people who are currently perhaps disenfranchised.

This particular headteacher was viewed by the local authority as being very successful and was widely respected for establishing strong links with the wider community.

The headteacher of Greville School had a similar community focus. He had a desire to involve others and to value their opinions and views, even when these views and opinions were critical:

I outlined my vision for the school and how I felt we needed to change in order to improve further and then I asked...[parents] for their views whether that fitted in with the way they were thinking, so we were talking about increased community provision on site, and more engagement with community and the parents were very positive and also very critical as well, they came up with some really good ideas.

He also revealed how he felt about members of his school and the community, explaining that 'everybody leads, everybody sets examples, and that's the way that is, that's the best way in my opinion in the circumstances that our school is in that you can bring about change and effect change'. Here the headteacher made reference to the importance, in schools in challenging circumstances, of all parties relaying a positive message as they are all responsible for instigating change and all have a leadership role. He made the point that the community had an influence on his students, but the students also had an influence on the community:

> We've done a lot of work on improving educational outcomes for students but there is a feeling that although we've done this work with them in the school once the students leave us and go into the community, what they are doing and how they spend their time is important in shaping that community.

Conclusions: Transformations and strategies

The headteachers in this study felt that their transformational leadership style was responsible for the successes they had in leading a school in challenging circumstances; specifically, it was perceived to be due to the headteachers' endeavours to alter the perceptions and self-belief of pupils, staff and members of the community. The headteachers believed strongly in a vision which was focused on changing the school ethos to empower students and raise aspirations. The involvement and development of followers was very important to headteachers in this initial study, as they felt their responsibility was to impact not only the students within their school but also the culture of the entire community. They approached this task by involving others in the creation and sharing of the vision, and nurturing a level of sustainability that would enable the vision to be communicated by more people. This was also seen as a means of inspiring others, by encouraging them to believe in an alternative future where their circumstances are improved, and where they are empowered to contribute towards bringing about this improvement.

The development of strong relationships was seen as crucial to success. Such relationships also enabled staff to adopt the organizational values set by the headteacher and carry these throughout the school, a view supported by MacBeath *et al.* (1996), who explain how staff work more effectively for the good of children when the headteacher is successful at empowering them and providing them with a sense of moral purpose. Bass and Steidlmeier (2006) argue that for leadership to be truly transformational it must be grounded in moral foundations, a criterion that was important for headteachers serving in these communities. They also point out that transformational leadership becomes values-driven leadership when the truth is told, when promises are kept, when negotiations are fair and choice is free (Bass and Steidlmeier, 2006). The headteachers in this study practised leadership based on the values of honesty, respect and trust (Cameron, 2006). They modelled their values for others to replicate in the way they fostered relationships and demonstrated a genuine belief in people, helping to raise the aspirations of others. The headteachers felt relationships were critical in schools situated in areas with high social deprivation, and the ability to form these relationships was a key to their success. They nurtured relationships between all members of the school as well as throughout the wider community, and they felt this generated instances of mutual respect, enabling the school to have a greater influence on the lives of others.

The link between values-driven leadership and transformational leadership is essential for these headteachers. Values and vision are critical ingredients for creating long-lasting, sustainable changes, as the leader's values become the principles on which the organization functions (Bellingham, 2003). The ability to create sustainable changes is one of the factors that encourages headteachers in these socially deprived communities to adopt a transformational style, and may indeed be a factor that encourages headteachers of this nature to work in schools situated in challenging circumstances. The desire that these headteachers possessed – wanting to make a difference by improving people's life-chances – lends itself to a socially deprived community where they can quickly see the impact of their actions. Similarly, the ability to see this impact encourages the headteachers to be transformational in their actions. It was noted that the newly appointed head of Blackwood School was, at the time of the interview, less transformational than the other headteachers in this study. This may be because headteachers become more transformational as they serve in a school in an area of high social deprivation, due to the constructivist paradigm. Such a shift may occur because the schools require that the headteacher becomes inspirational and maintains a positive attitude that, in turn, leads to the manifestation of the headteacher's desired vision. This may take place because the headteachers ground themselves in their fundamental values, searching for fairness and equality for members of community in challenging circumstances. The headteachers feel morally bound to provide the best options possible for members of the community, which then enables them to achieve even greater successes, helping realize their vision and reinforce their desire to help more people. When heads are able to pursue their own moral purpose in interactions with others, their own energy levels and long-term effectiveness cease to become depleted (Hargreaves and Fink, 2007).

6

Implementing Transformational Leadership in a Challenging School: A Case Study

This chapter marks the turning point from theoretical research to its practical application. The deputy head of one of the four schools in challenging circumstances which were the subject of the original leadership research study was appointed to a headship. Although the new school was in a different local authority, there were many parallels with the challenging circumstances found in Coalborough, including many of the same problems, and the newly appointed headteacher decided that he wished to implement the results of the Coalborough work with his new colleagues and students at Packwood School.

So far, different types of leadership styles have been considered and the ways in which they might be relevant to educational institutions have been examined. The main focus has been on aspects of transactional and transformational leadership, identifying the strategies deployed by four headteachers, especially in the area of transformational leadership. The study has established that transformational leadership in schools is based on establishing and communicating a clear vision based on espoused values. Leadership has to be shared. Motivating and empowering staff is essential and has to be linked to professional and personal development, which enables colleagues to take responsibility for their own actions and become more creative in their work. The benefits of both transactional and transformational leadership to the running of schools have been examined, identifying the possible links these styles have to a constructivist paradigm in order to create a reality that is manifested through absolute belief. The work described in this book was carried out in socially and economically challenged areas in the north of England, in schools and locations which have been given pseudonyms for the purposes of this volume. The original research, phase one, was carried out in four schools in the town of Coalborough, a former mining community. The results were subsequently implemented at Packwood School, which, although situated in Willbridge, a separate local authority also in the north of England, shares many of the social and educational characteristics of the original sample.

Packwood School: The background

Willbridge is considerably larger than Coalborough, with 47 secondary schools, and covers a much larger area with a more diverse spread of achievements. Ofsted described this diversity when they wrote that it:

> serves a county of contrasts with a wide span of advantage and disadvantage. Unemployment is broadly in line with the national average, but this masks significant disparities at district and ward level. The regeneration of the county from its former coalmining and manufacturing base has been a priority for the council, and building thriving communities, raising educational achievement and promoting social inclusion are rightly seen as crucial to the necessary process of social and economic regeneration.

> (OFSTED, 2003)

In 2010, the highest performing school in Willbridge local authority achieved 80 percent five A* to C grades, including English and Maths, whereas the lowest performing school achieved 30 percent, with Packwood School scoring 31 percent, placing it in the bottom three schools in the authority. This achievement was 20 percent below the Authority Average, which in turn was 2 percent below the National Average. By 2011, just before the current head was appointed, Packwood School was in the bottom four schools in Willbridge local authority, achieving 41 percent five A* to Cs, whereas the highest performing school in the authority achieved 90 percent; the Authority Average for this year was within 1 percent of the National Average of 58 percent. Although the authority can now be considered to be in line with the National Average, Packwood School is situated in a specific region of Willbridge, a former mining area where every secondary school has been categorized by Ofsted as underperforming. Of these, Packwood School was the lowest performing school and the only one to be placed into special measures.

Packwood School was created in 2004 when two underachieving schools were merged. It has about 1,500 students (200 of whom are in the sixth form) and has a long history of underachievement. It was hoped that the better of the two schools, which itself was categorized by Ofsted as having serious weaknesses, would help lift the other school out of special measures. Instead, the entire newly merged school was eventually classified by Ofsted as inadequate and placed in special measures. During its time under special measures, it had three different headteachers.

A comparison of the 2009 figures for Packwood School with those for the schools which took part in the original phase one research (Table 1.1) places Packwood below them, with a five A* to C including English and Maths achievement of just 26 percent. At this time, Ofsted provided the following description of Packwood School's context:

> The school serves the southern part of [a town within Willbridge local authority] and outlying villages, many of which were mining communities until recently. There is considerable social and economic deprivation affecting some of these communities. The attainment of pupils on entry to the school is below average. The proportion of pupils eligible for free school meals is above average, as is the proportion of pupils with learning difficulties.
>
> (OFSTED, 2006)

In March 2010, the Ofsted report introduction made direct references to the problems identified as significant factors associated with recruiting staff within schools in challenging circumstances, stating:

> In the last academic year, there were several long-term staff absences, including those of a number of senior leaders, and the school had difficulties in recruiting and retaining staff in English, mathematics and special educational needs.
>
> (OFSTED, 2010)

In 2011, under the previous headteacher, Packwood School improved by 10 percent to reach 41 percent of students achieving five A* to C including English and Maths, which still placed it within the bottom five schools in this authority. Packwood School has reduced in numbers since falling into special measures and currently has 1,404 students on roll, down from 1,529 the previous year. The school had been in special measures for 18 months when a new headteacher was appointed in January 2011. This headteacher, Dr Hurst, had formerly been a deputy at one of the schools which took part in the original, phase one research study of headteacher leadership in challenging circumstances. Since the new head has been in post, there has been one inspection by Ofsted, which stated that the school was no longer failing and was satisfactory in all categories. Ofsted described the school thus:

> Most students are White British. There is a smaller than national proportion of students who are from minority ethnic groups or who speak English as an additional language. The proportion of students who are known to be eligible for free school meals is above the national average. The proportion of disabled students and those with special educational needs is above the national average. At its previous inspection in 2010, the school was judged to require special measures.

(OFSTED, 2012)

Packwood School's results have never previously met the targets set. These targets are based on the prior attainment of students entering the school and the expected progress that students of this level would be expected to achieve in other schools. However, 2012 saw a dramatic improvement of 16 percent, meaning that the school not only achieved its targets but also exceeded them, placing its performance in the top 25 percent of all schools nationally (see Table 6.1 and Appendix 3). It is clear from this table, however, that Packwood has consistently fallen below national and local authority averages for GCSE results and that this trend continued in 2012, in spite of the improvements made. Although Packwood is now much closer to the national average, there is still some way to go to raise performance above the local authority average, which has itself risen by 15.3 percent over this period.

The second part of the work described in this volume began two years after the end of the initial phase one research study, when Dr Hurst embarked upon his first headship at Packwood School. As has already been noted, this

TABLE 6.1 The percentage of five A* to C GCSE grades achieved by Packwood School compared with local and national averages

	2009	2010	2011	2012
Packwood School (%)	26	31	41	57
LA average (%)	47.2	51.4	57.6	62.5
National average (%)	49.8	53.5	59	59.4

Source: © Crown copyright 2012 (http://www.education.gov.uk) (the school unique reference number has been anonymized).

was also a school in challenging circumstances with many similarities to the Coalborough schools where he had been a deputy. Dr Hurst had followed the progress and results of the initial research with great interest and told the researchers of his decision to attempt to implement transformational leadership methods at Packwood, his new school. It was decided to use Packwood as an implementation study extending the original research and using, as far as possible, the same research methods.

First impressions of Packwood School

Willbridge local authority is considerably larger than Coalborough, where the phase one schools were located, although, as has been noted, it also serves a former mining area. The data in this chapter were collected after Dr Hurst's first year in post. The case study of the implementation of the findings of the main study was necessarily undertaken in a slightly different way to phase one, but built upon the findings from the original study. This implementation case study looks at the leadership style adopted by a headteacher who is fully aware of the research of phase one, and who took a conscious approach to develop the findings on transformational aspects of leadership in an attempt to employ the proposals from the original research and identify the impact these would have on a failing school situated in challenging circumstances. Much of the case study data were collected during interviews with Dr Hurst. However, greater understanding is gained from the latest Ofsted report, which is included to provide an external measure of possible improvements. Following this latest Ofsted report, subsequent examination results provide statistical data that are used to generate qualitative measures of possible improvements. In addition to this, the school administrative staff sent out questionnaires to students, staff, parents and governors, 45 of which were returned and analysed to find if the perception of improvement at Packwood was shared by other stakeholders. The research team was also given access to approximately 50 unsolicited emails and letters sent to the school and use was also made of articles in the local press.

This chapter follows Dr Hurst's initial year as a headteacher, depicting his experiences and interpretations, achievements and failures, analysing how these changes have occurred and attempting to map the actions onto the areas identified earlier as those of transformational leaders. Similarities are drawn between the aspects of transformational leadership in theory and the practices that have been implemented at Packwood School. As in the phase one research, the majority of evidence comes directly from the headteacher as he set about attempting to change Packwood School. This was brought about by the deliberate application of the transformational strategies that were identified in the first part of this study. However, as the evidence collected from the heads of the four schools in the earlier research showed, both transformational leadership and transactional leadership tend to be necessary, with transformational leadership bringing about school-wide improvements and transactional leadership ensuring that policy and procedures are followed.

Dr Hurst took up his post in January 2011. It was his first headship. He was asked to describe what the school was like when he first arrived. He started by stating baldly: 'It was the worst school I had ever seen.' He described the level of despair he had witnessed in the school, with students openly breaking rules in front of staff and staff feeling that they could not challenge the behaviour, as there was too much to deal with. He talked about children setting off fire alarms, sometimes up to three times a day, and kicking doors off their hinges. He recalled the chaos and lack of regard for others and how distressing he had found this:

> It is a two-storey school with balconies where students would stand pouring orange juice onto passers-by. On some occasions students would hang and drop between floors rather than use the stairs. It was a very menacing place where you felt unsafe just being around the site; in my first two weeks here, I personally was assaulted on more than one occasion, and saw other teachers being pushed, sworn at, and having things thrown at them. The playground was dangerous, and I saw a child ride his bike through the playground at lunchtime, hitting lots of children and knocking them out of the way, enjoying hurting them. There were lots of no-go areas for teachers, and when the bells went to signify that lessons were starting, nobody moved, instead they just stayed in their groups socializing or smoking. Teachers told me one of their biggest problems were the hordes of students in corridors during lesson time. These students would open classroom doors, interrupt lessons and shout to friends across classrooms, but as they weren't supposed to be in that lesson, the teachers didn't know the students and didn't feel confident in dealing with them. The school had been in special measures for two years, and showed no sign of coming out.

Comparing this initial impression with the school as it was two terms later, it was apparent that there had been a remarkable turnaround. Within two terms, under the transformational leadership model, the school was removed from special measures, converted into an academy and achieved the highest results ever recorded for the school, or indeed for the two previous schools. The results were dramatically improved in all measures, from the National Measures of attainment to the amount of progress that students made from entering to leaving the school. Analysis of the results also revealed that all groups of children, including those with Special Educational Needs and Disabilities, receiving free school meals, vulnerable students, and both gender groups, had made significant progress (Appendix 2). In addition to this, other measures revealed a perception of improvement even before the examination results were published; this was evident from the questionnaires given to staff, to students and to governors, all of which revealed that 100 percent of respondents felt that the school had improved significantly. Of the questionnaires given to parents, only one parent did not feel that it had improved significantly; the school was aware of this parent's concern and was dealing with an ongoing issue that had originated prior to the new head's arrival.

Dr Hurst was asked whether becoming an academy had been significant in the improvement process, and how it had impacted on the school, and he provided an overview of the process and the reasons behind becoming an academy. The latter included a long history of underperformance from the school, resulting in special measures with no visible method of escaping this underachievement. The local authority had taken several courses of action, including amalgamating two schools, investing over £30 million in building a new school and replacing the leadership team, but the school had still remained failing. It was true that these initiatives did have an impact, generating the school's highest results ever of 41 percent five A* to C including English and Maths. However, after exhausting every avenue, the results had plateaued at 15 percent below the target figure, and there was no apparent means of generating any further improvement.

It was Dr Hurst's understanding that the local authority approached a chain of academies with a reputation for improving schools. Converting to academies had become a national topic and had the political backing of the government. Converting the school to an academy was a quick way of handing over the school's governance to the chain, although in reality the schools involved in this chain had already worked with other schools before the academy conversion programme came into existence. He explained how Packwood School had adopted the overall vision for that group of academies based on 'putting students first'. In his opinion, however, although the academies programme had served as a vehicle for this change, it was not directly responsible for it:

> As an academy chain, we believe very strongly in maintaining as many of the benefits that already exist. For example, we don't break away from the local authority, but instead subscribe to maintain their services and make full use of these. We also maintain all the teachers' pay and conditions, so teachers don't notice any changes to their employment. More importantly, although academies can be selective in the students they accept, we never are; we maintain the same catchment area and view ourselves as fully comprehensive.

The process of change:
Transforming the transactional

Dr Hurst pointed out that at Packwood School transactional leadership was now used at every level from quality assurance systems to self-evaluation, and from creating duty rotas to evidencing criteria for Ofsted. The headteacher followed a policy of tempering any duties that demanded transactional styles of leadership by shaping them, as far as possible, to also include transformational aspects that develop and motivate. He provided an example of this:

> Take for example, something such as the Performance Management cycle that all schools follow. This is naturally transactional in its definition as people are given a series of targets to meet in order to receive pay progression. However, the manner in which these meetings are undertaken, and the tracking used, does not have to be transactional at all. If the Performance Management meetings are approached from a place where the reviewer is intent on praising, providing challenge and inspiring the reviewee, then the Performance Management meeting can continue to serve the development of the school. I feel that this was the original purpose of this system, but as too often happens it becomes a tick-box exercise where people complete the minimum requirements to just get it done. By approaching all transactional duties with the view that they will continue to serve the development of individuals, then they don't have to undermine your overall vision.

This is consistent with the description in phase one, where leaders were able to mediate policy through their own value systems. Dr Hurst applied a similar philosophy to writing reports for Ofsted, describing how it can be used as an opportunity to discuss the personal achievements of individuals and to reflect on their growth, while simultaneously providing an opening to strengthen and clarify the school's vision. He argued that every transactional role provides chances for staff development and by focusing more on this, rather than on the duty itself, the transactional duties become just another vehicle to accelerate change:

> I did a staff training session entitled *Connecting to the Purpose*. In this session I discussed the importance of being in the right paradigm when we undertake school roles. I even went on to cite staff break-time duties and how it is possible to stand on duty resenting the time wasted and making no difference to the school. When the duty is completed in this frame of mind it provides no benefit to anyone, and can even have a very negative

impact on the person doing the duty. However, if you approach this in an active manner, circulating amongst students, smiling and connecting with them, then not only do you complete your duty more effectively, but you also create a better ethos for the school, gain a reputation of being a sound teacher, and become a more effective classroom practitioner by knowing students better.

This training session also included references to how to undertake many mundane tasks that some teachers find draining. One example was that of marking books. He described how he had detailed the different ways by which people undertake this. Some approach this with the mind-set of it being a chore, and by doing this it does become a chore; it is very time-consuming and produces a negative effect, having no overall impact. The time spent marking in this way really is wasted. However, when you connect to the purpose, you find that you do a much better job. Firstly, it becomes something you want to do, rather than a chore, and you enjoy the time you get to spend looking at what students have produced; it becomes delightful to see students apply their teachings and achieve. Also, your written comments reflect this. They automatically become more personalized and motivating. The outcome is that you actually achieve many more benefits by investing this small amount of time. Instead of it being a drain, it becomes an effective use of time, producing good outputs for a little input. He concluded that this rule of 'connecting to the purpose' always empowered teachers and created a shared vision of accomplishment, where teachers had higher levels of morale and enjoyed their work more. Dr Hurst maintained, therefore, that any transactional role can have transformational outcomes, provided it is approached in the correct manner.

Change through transformational leadership strategies

Dr Hurst was asked to summarize the things he does as a leader that he feels created the transformation at Packwood. His responses reflected the findings of the study of the four headteachers in the original Coalborough study, although his initial position seems to belie this. He said that good leadership was very simple and one should try hard not to overcomplicate it. This is an insight that is surprisingly uncommon in educational institutions. Dr Hurst argued that good leadership firstly relies on a strong, clear vision where the school, and every individual in the school, improves. This vision needs to be shared as often as possible, with as many people as possible, and should centre on a few key words or key phrases that others start to pick up on and carry with them, phrases like 'Connect to the Purpose', 'Students First' or 'Our Journey to Outstanding'. Following on from this, the actions that leaders take must show that the leader believes in the vision and expects it to manifest itself in action. Secondly, leaders must invest heavily in people; offering training, support, mentoring and their time. Colleagues must be provided with challenges constantly, pushing them to improve and helping them form their own foundation of values, ones that guide them to becoming the person they were meant to be. Finally, never accept any excuse. When a leader joins a failing school, that leader hears everyone's excuses for failure. Most of these are valid and absolutely true to the people reporting them. From the community the school serves to the lack of support for the school from external agencies, from the layout or size of the school to over-inflated entry grades or even claims of vindictive Ofsted inspectors – leaders will hear them all, and as the leader of the school, the new headteacher has to make it clear that no excuse is ever good enough to prevent achievement. What is more, new leaders have to be completely optimistic in their approach to dispelling these excuses, and know that all the research into failing schools is done in schools that are different from this one. In other words, what new leaders will be faced with in failing schools and in schools in challenging circumstances is a process of denial. Hence, it is important that new leaders write their own story, change the focus from reasons for failure and concentrate on strategies for success.

The changes that Dr Hurst initiated at Packwood School were based on a conscious decision to use transformational leadership as a vehicle for change to accelerate improvements within the school. He recognized that this would require a heavy investment in staff training: two hours were spent every week developing teams and securing consistency. Training was sometimes used for whole school sessions and sometimes for departmental activities. Whole school sessions included effective planning, dealing with poor behaviour and setting a vision for improvement. The focus was on making lessons enjoyable, engaging students and ensuring progress. This training was supported by informal mentoring and coaching. The departmental-level training sessions for heads of department, run by the headteacher, covered ways to continually improve: securing staff commitment, managing time, being a good leader, ensuring quality, target setting and achievement and interventions that make a difference. Within departments, training sessions dealt with topics such as standardizing marking, collaborative planning and literacy in your subject. All of this activity was based on shared values such as putting the student first and never giving up on a student. It was important for staff not to hold grudges, and each student was to be given a clean slate once a sanction had been served.

When asked about the ways this vision was shared, the headteacher explained:

At one of the first sessions I explained what the SLT [Senior Leadership Team] would do to support staff, and promised that students would not get into their lessons if they were out of uniform. At the time, I noticed lots of staff look at each other, as if to imply that that was impossible, which was understandable as it was hard to find a student with their tie on, or shirt tucked in – and in fact one Vice Principal told me that was almost all he did all day, focus on uniform. To change this, we had all SLT out on the gate at 7.50am before the start of day at 8.25. Anyone not in uniform was loaned the correct uniform and given a detention for being out of uniform. This now means you cannot see a single student out of uniform anywhere in the school, and teachers can focus their time on real priorities, such as the quality of learning.

The emphasis on school uniform was deliberate. In one sense, school uniform was a symbolic representation of much that was wrong with Packwood. Wearing the correct uniform was a school rule that was deliberately, consistently and visibly flaunted. The breach of this rule was easy to identify, and its enforcement was relatively simple. Dr Hurst noted that he received lots of complaints from parents, all of whom had valid reasons for their child being out of uniform. He stated that he would never back down. He pointed out that this helped show students rules would be enforced and that parental comments could not overrule the school rules. This was a big change, since previously students had been able to tell their parents and punishments had been dropped if parents argued on their child's behalf.

If the enforcement of the school rule about wearing uniforms was symbolic, changing behaviour in classrooms was practical. It is widely recognized that one of the most difficult things for any headteacher to achieve is to influence what goes on once the classroom door has closed. Dr Hurst argued that to achieve changes in the classroom, it was necessary to focus both on consistency, in terms of what behaviour was acceptable and what was not, and on the individual interactions between staff and students. The starting point was student behaviour, both inside and outside the classroom. Students had previously hidden in stairwells and on the playing fields to avoid lessons. The tracking system for identifying which students should be in which lesson was improved and rigorously applied. Senior staff started to ensure that students were in lessons by patrolling the corridors, and the head banned the use of the extensive playing field for anything other than teaching purposes during the school day. To support the school, the local authority has now started to issue fixed penalty truancy notices to the parents of students who do not attend school. Damage to the school building has also decreased. When Dr Hurst became head, a small team of maintenance staff was kept busy on a permanent basis repairing doors, removing graffiti and dealing with a wide range of deliberate damage; this is now unnecessary. The false fire alarms that plagued the school, sometimes as many as three times a day, have stopped, and behaviour in the classrooms has also improved.

Staff were told to use a 'three ticks and you are out' approach to poor behaviour. This meant that any student receiving more than three reprimands for poor behaviour or being late for lessons would be removed from the classroom to an isolation room staffed by a member of SLT and given detention. Initially, there would be up to 40 students removed each period, all of whom received a follow-up detention. Currently, there are about eight such students each day. This is still too many, but it is a great improvement. The SLT was scheduled to meet families and students who were underachieving due to poor behaviour. The purpose of these meetings was to describe the changes that were taking place, to ensure that rules were understood and to make clear the expectations that the school now had of its students.

The SLT was instructed never to compromise when meeting students and families, but instead to insist on absolute compliance with the new systems. Dr Hurst stated that this was a lot of short-term pain for long-term gains. For many members of the SLT, this was very difficult and they had to be reminded daily to 'hold the line' and centre on the vision of what the school wants ultimately, rather than on where they were at present. He highlighted the need for consistency in everything in order to bring about quick changes, stating that a lack of consistency would undermine everything and slow down any progress. He drew attention to the manner in which this was applied to students and also to staff, allowing no room for deviation:

> We made sure rules and expectations were very clear, shared these with governors, parents, staff and students, and also made it clear that deviations from this would not be allowed. So students had clear guidelines on behaviour and the consequences for not adhering to these. Also teachers had a level of consistency that they had to adhere to. Some felt this stripped away their professionalism, and wanted more freedom. With this in mind, the vision had to be very simple and clear, making sure everyone knew we are a united team all driving towards excellence and never settling for underachievement wherever it is found. When the teachers saw how the changes we were making would benefit children, giving them greater chances in life and preparing them for a lifetime of success, then most came on board.

Not everyone, however, supported the attempts to improve student behaviour. Some parents were difficult and reluctant to accept any changes, accusing the school in the local press of treating students like criminals. Although these parents knew the school was failing, and said that they wanted it to improve, they were against any changes that impacted them directly. When pushed for an example, the headteacher shared one of the most extreme:

> There's one family whose child constantly receives punishments for bullying others or purposely disrupting lessons. He is very clear about the rules and chooses to devote his time to upsetting others. The child's behaviour is very extreme and is completely unacceptable. However, his family refuse to let the child have any form of punishment, to such an extent that they have complained to the local MP, written to the newspapers, and started their own Facebook campaign against the school. The really negative aspect of this is that the Facebook comments are full of lies and are open to be viewed by anyone, with friends and family members of these parents adding to the comments and fuelling the lies. As Facebook is pretty much unregulated, we can't refute these and others read them and start to believe them.

Many more parents, however, supported the school. Some would openly state in meetings how pleased they were with the changes and the leadership of the school, but these parents are not the type to publish their views on the Internet. Consequently, what happens, Dr Hurst argued, is the school's bad press perpetuates longer than it should and, as a result, has a negative impact on the achievements of the school. Because Packwood had always had a poor reputation, this would not improve until it was widely recognized that student behaviour had improved, and would continue to improve, through the consistent implementation of school rules. Nevertheless, the school's reputation is improving. Staff at a local bank commented that until recently customers remained inside the bank at the end of the school day to avoid the Packwood students. This no longer happens and the students are polite and friendly. The head of a secondary school in a nearby city who happens to live near Packwood School recently wrote to Dr Hurst complimenting him on the improvement in student behaviour in the town. A primary school head sent a similar letter. Rigorous and consistent enforcement of simple rules seems to have been the key to this improvement.

Consistency within the school applied not only to student behaviour but also to teaching. Dr Hurst argued that there was little point in ensuring that students attended lessons and improved their behaviour if lessons were not engaging. Consistency for teachers in their classrooms included common structures for sharing learning outcomes, common practices for changing between activities, common procedures for engaging students in discussions and common routines for encouraging students to accept challenging tasks. These common routines included a structured approach to lesson planning and delivery, which was outlined by Dr Hurst. At the start of each lesson, the learning outcomes for the session are written on the board. Teachers must introduce the lesson, referring to the outcomes and how they will be achieved. The tasks must be meaningful, relevant and constructive. At the same time, changes were made to the curriculum, especially the option blocks. Options start in Year 9, and each student selects two options for a year, so students take six options by the end of Year 11 (see Appendix 3). Packwood School has now moved away from fixed-option blocks. Instead, a full range of choices is given to students and the blocks are then fixed around student choices; if enough students choose an option, it runs. This means that departments have to consider carefully what options they can and do offer and at what levels. They must give students advice and guidance about what choices are best for them (not for the teacher or the department). The head noted that experienced teachers felt that all of this was a big change, especially if they viewed themselves as successful teachers. It was stressed, however, that this consistency would empower all teachers, providing frameworks where students knew and responded to routines.

A great deal of training and support was needed to ensure consistency and to encourage reluctant teachers to embrace the new changes. Dr Hurst maintained that one of the most important aspects of implementing this change was to lead by example; it was imperative therefore that he not only delivered this training session personally, but also taught within the school. The headteacher stressed that this meant other teachers could see him practise what he preached. Teachers would hear students comment on how enjoyable his lessons were and how much they were achieving, compared with their previous teaching. In addition to this, Dr Hurst actively looked for teachers embracing these changes and then had them present their experiences at staff briefing meetings, providing testimonials as to how their lessons had improved by trying these new structures. He provided examples of how this was done:

> As we walked the academy, we would see a teacher who had some great learning outcomes and had chosen some exciting activities as a way of teaching the material. We would ask this teacher to talk to staff about how he had planned and delivered this lesson, and how students had really enjoyed it and engaged. We would ask several teachers to do this, always where we had noticed a buzz of excitement from students. When this was shared with staff, others would see how teachers were able to take risks by trying something new, and more importantly how students had responded well to this. The idea was to show staff that if you take the time to prepare something good for students, then they will engage more and won't let you down like they used to.

Dr Hurst commented that staff morale was now extremely high and that staff absence had improved to such an extent that in many weeks there was no staff absence. This had not happened at Packwood before. Furthermore, there are now no members of staff on long-term sick leave. When Dr Hurst took over, there were a number on more or less permanent absence for sickness. He did note that while most staff supported the changes that he was bringing about, not all staff were fully engaged. He explained that the vast majority of staff were excited about the journey they were taking. He gave examples of teachers who had 'upped their game' and become real leaders, both within the school and within their departments, sharing examples of many who had expressed their appreciation of the quality of support they were receiving and the attitude of the students in their lessons. The headteacher stated that, as in all schools, there are always some staff who are relatively behind others in their development. Many of these colleagues were continuing to improve, and it was hoped that their achievements would fuel greater progress.

Dr Hurst did admit, however, that there were some staff who will not or do not wish to improve their professional practice. He explained that these fell into two main categories: some who feel that the pace and challenge of the school is too much for them and others who should not be in the teaching profession. The head described how the first of these groups had already started to apply to leave and join other schools, and noted that the training these staff had received at Packwood had developed them so they were in a better position to apply for other jobs. He cited a few staff who had received promotions in other schools, stressing how they would continue to receive his full support. The second group, he declared, are those who should not be in teaching:

Some teachers lose their way and forget how important their role is. I don't feel they are always to blame for this; sometimes they work in an environment where bad habits are the norm, and under such conditions it is difficult to stay connected to your purpose. Here we have seen many staff re-ignited when reminded of their purpose and provided with the tools and support to achieve it. Although, for a small minority, it is a bridge too far. There are very clear systems in place for staff like these, and what we do is continue to provide high levels of training and support, but never accept substandard performance. We set clear, achievable goals and always hold on to the hope that these teachers will rise to the acceptable standard, but know that there is an alternative route if the teacher's capability is in question. We must always remember that schools are about students being given life-chances, and although we achieve this by empowering and developing staff, we never make the mistake of thinking a school is here to give jobs to staff, because it isn't.

Dr Hurst went on to report some verbal feedback from the lead Ofsted inspector when the school was brought out of special measures. This inspector stated that it was unusual to see so many changes implemented in such a short time, and yet there was a lack of change-fatigue. Ofsted commented that their findings were that people were supporting the changes and that staff and student morale were really high, with everyone clear about what they were intending on achieving and how they were going to do it.

Many of the changes that Dr Hurst and his staff initiated took place in parallel. Dr Hurst argued that if he had tried to implement changes one by one, then it would have taken far too long for there to be any noticeable improvement at Packwood School. Many of these first-order issues were so serious that the problems needed to be tackled at the same time. To some extent, the changes in pupil behaviour, wearing of school uniform, pedagogy and staff self-motivation complemented each other – making a virtue out of necessity. These changes had been brought about by focusing on two main areas that Dr Hurst felt had needed changing: the label that everyone carried with them of being failing, and the self-belief (or lack of it) that people had. He addressed these two issues by focusing on standards and creating a vision of what could be possible – a vision made up of very small changes, but leading to large, tangible improvements.

If Dr Hurst's first priority in bringing about change at Packwood School was behaviour in all of its forms, then his second priority for change was that of raising the self-belief of individuals. He explained how he had managed to raise aspirations and ambition by constantly painting a vision of a brighter future that everyone felt was possible. This was originally done through assemblies, meetings and interactions with individuals, but then expanded into tutor-group work which students and their tutors would undertake together, giving them ownership of the vision and a clear pathway for bringing about changes. He went right back to basics in his interactions, spelling out how children should develop a sense of integrity and self-worth, providing concrete examples of what students should do in their daily practices in order to build these values and how they would know if they were on the right track. One of the assemblies delivered was entitled 'It costs too much' and spelt out how making wrong choices, and taking the easiest path, can often have lasting implications that cost people more in the longer term. This was then followed up throughout the week with students reflecting on their previous actions and identifying where they had made poor choices. The next day they created a plan of how they would act in future when similar circumstances arose. The headteacher said this was done to help them form a blueprint for their actions, and also to encourage them to start seeing themselves as value-driven people who are aware of their actions and the consequences of these, making conscious decisions towards improvement. He declared that instilling values and self-worth into students was fundamental, in his view, for ensuring they had a strong self-belief and could start to set and realize high aspirations.

Staff self-belief was equally important for Dr Hurst. He pointed out that he initiated 'a massive push on building capacity among staff'. He outlined how he had encouraged staff to start taking risks and have greater faith in their abilities. In the beginning, staff felt paralysed to act without first seeking approval from the head. He shared his judgment that staff felt fearful that their actions may be seen as wrong and they would be disciplined or overruled for even the smallest things. He changed this perception by making sure it was seen that teachers received the full backing of the headteacher, and if they had made a sound decision, then the headteacher would support them even if things went wrong to ensure their decisions led to successes. Many staff were shocked and surprised at the beginning when the headteacher sided with them over complaining parents, an outcome they were not used to. He explained why this was the case:

> I think that the school was underperforming so much, that nobody had faith in their actions, and so when questioned about anything they simply changed. Parents had developed a practice of always complaining to the headteacher whenever their child received a sanction, such as a detention from a member of staff. At the beginning, this was very difficult to change, with parents feeling that I was unfair to insist that their child complete the detention for the teacher, when they were fully aware that many other students had done much worse behaviour and not been punished in the past. By holding the line very strongly, the attitude of parents began to change and they started to realize that the systems were fair in their implementation and every child who behaved in a particular way would always receive the same punishment. This empowered staff to also hold the line, and now it has completely changed, with receptionists informing parents that, although they can talk to a senior member of staff should they insist on doing so, there is still an awareness that the sanction will not be cancelled.

The empowerment fostered a belief among the staff that the headteacher respected their professionalism and encouraged them to take greater risks in the classroom, secure in the knowledge that misbehaviour from students would never be tolerated. To achieve this, Dr Hurst spent time in lessons with students and with teachers, praising them for the way they embraced the new classroom structures. Really good teaching practitioners were asked to lead small sections of staff-briefing meetings, or to deliver at staff-training sessions. When teachers stood up and shared details of how they were changing and how this had led to positive achievements, other staff started discussing the implementation more. In addition, the relationship between staff changed, with more people praising each other and asking for or offering advice. This led to a small initiative which indicated that staff were starting to believe; some members of staff approached the headteacher with a request for a new school-wide system of 'wild-cards', where staff would stick a wild-card to their classroom door to inform other staff that they were attempting something out of their comfort zone. The card served two purposes: first to say, please call into my room and see what I am doing – offering support if possible – and secondly to say 'don't judge me, I am trying something new'. In one 'wild-card' case, a business studies teacher developed activities similar to the television business programme *Dragon's Den* as a way of teaching the curriculum. He shared his planning, delivery and assessment ideas with the rest of the staff. On another occasion, a technology teacher tried using 'memory material', where students created something new that they could take home. One of the Vice Principals commented that 'There was a buzz of excitement about the classroom so I asked the teacher to share her ideas with the rest of the staff, especially how she had taken a risk by trying something new.'

The head described these examples as just small indications that staff were embracing their new challenges and becoming leaders in their own right. Based around this, the headteacher asked staff to leave their classrooms and go and see someone else teach, even if it were just for five minutes during their non-contact time. The level of change that this brought should not be underestimated; discussions between staff changed to become focused on the quality of learning and the high levels of provision that students receive. There developed an ethos of professional respect between teachers and this created a team with drive, rather than individuals struggling in isolation with classroom problems.

Changes to staff and student behaviour, teaching and self-belief were accompanied by changes to the work of the SLT, as senior leaders within the school also went through a paradigm shift. Dr Hurst recalled how members of the SLT would previously spend hours on administration tasks and hold meetings that had nothing to do with school improvement – actions the headteacher felt had been their way of working towards some small achievement within a failing school. He explained how he had to refocus the senior staff to concentrate on the important issues, so they could become a driving force for change. To begin with, the SLT had to focus on discipline. Senior leaders were instructed never to use their offices during the school day. Instead, they should spend their time throughout the school and in lessons, supporting teachers and working with students. Administration duties needed to be minimized, as most such tasks did not have a sufficient impact on the achievement of students. Devoting the time to interacting with students would produce more important results. Any administrative duties or meetings that were absolutely essential needed to take place out of learning time. Both senior leaders and teachers were unused to this and felt very uncomfortable at the start, so much so that the leadership team were apprehensive about entering a classroom when a teacher was teaching. To embed this practice, the headteacher devoted an hour of every Senior Leadership Meeting to feedback from the team on the week's interactions within lessons. This was then followed up by praise being given to the teachers who had been discussed at the meetings. The headteacher felt that this helped build the vision for the school, as he was able to voice his pleasure when Senior Leaders talked about classroom practices that they felt were worthy of note. This also implied that the Leadership Team were more aware of their school, and carried with them an idea of the good lessons that were taking place, as well as ideas on how to improve other lessons. One of the Vice Principals stated that the changes in the school were so extreme that it was like comparing night and day. Instead of devoting all his time to tackling minutiae, he was now a strategic leader, with an awareness of where the school was and what was needed to do to move it to where they want it to be. He said he would have claimed to have been able to do this before, but now was fully aware that he was previously lacking in these skills. Another Vice Principal described how this had been the best year of her career, going so far as to describe her experiences as 'amazing'. She went on to state how the school was now a great place to work and how she felt enabled to 'just get on with it'.

Dr Hurst also created processes to include more and more staff in the leadership of the school. He described how the weekly staff training sessions had been expanded to include contributions from an increasing number of individuals. Such improvements had been achieved by:

> providing a great deal of staff training and personal coaching. At the beginning I delivered the first few training sessions myself, then expanded this to include the Vice-Principals, and now we have NQTs and other enthusiastic teachers contributing. There's now also a team of staff who are fully in charge of staff training and feel empowered to make important decisions about the training we need and the quality of training they are willing to accept. Quite often they ask to quality assure the things I intend delivering and they make positive changes to ensure the impact is maximized; we are now a real team with everyone on the same side. We've even expanded this so that students deliver INSET to staff.

The headteacher recalled how he knew the staff developments he was hoping for were being realized when a group of Heads of Department approached him and asked if he would meet them one morning each fortnight, to provide coaching and mentoring sessions on personal improvement. This was an opportunity to empower leaders to carry out changes within their departments. These sessions started off with the head sharing ideas and educational practices on topics such as how to hold staff to account, how to make empowering decisions and how to model success. The sessions evolved into a discussion group and are now a self-improvement group, where the head just contributes while others take the leadership role, discussing ways of improving the school, sharing best practice and having greater impact from their actions. The head was extremely pleased with this outcome; he perceived this to be the start of a self-evolving school that will far exceed his original vision. He explained how talented these Heads of Department were and how he was often in awe of their contributions; they possess skills that he felt had been suppressed, without a forum to surface or an opportunity to discuss them. Dr Hurst argued that once these skills had been revealed and harnessed, significant contributions were made to tangible outcomes within Packwood School.

Changes resulting from academy status

Packwood School became an academy part way through Dr Hurst's first year in post. Prior to his appointment, Dr Hurst noted that Packwood School had a long history of underperformance, resulting in the school entering special measures. The local authority had taken several courses of action, including amalgamating two schools, investing over £30 million in building a new school, and replacing the leadership team, but the school still continued to fail and, although there was some small but insufficient improvement, remained failing. The local authority then approached a chain of academies with a reputation for improving schools. Converting the school to an academy seemed to be a quick way of handing over the school's governance and its problems to a particular academy group that had already worked with other schools in the authority. Once part of the academy group, Packwood School adopted the overall vision for that group of academies based on 'Putting students first'. Dr Hurst argued that although the academies programme had served as a vehicle for this change it was not directly responsible for it. This academy group believes very strongly in maintaining as many local contacts as possible. Consequently, Packwood School remains fully comprehensive.

Dr Hurst was asked to estimate how much of the recent success of the school could be accredited to the academy model. He emphasized that not all academy models are the same, and added that he felt privileged to be part of a particular family of schools. The family of schools of which Packwood was a part was, in his opinion, very different from other academy chains, some of which were, in his opinion, 'hungry for schools' and snapped up as many as possible. This academy chain, however, only had a few schools and was reluctant to expand until each of the schools was outstanding. He did not believe that it was the 'academy' label that made a difference to the school, but the philosophy of the academy chain leaders. It was Dr Hurst's view that the academy system generally provided an umbrella that allowed changes to occur rapidly, as everyone expected to see changes when a school became an academy. The changes that had occurred at Packwood, however, were those that would have taken place anyway, irrespective of its status – academy or not. Asked if he perceived any advantages to becoming an academy, Dr Hurst replied that apart from the greater freedom, most of the advantages simply accrued from being part of that particular family of schools, rather than being an academy:

> As part of a family of schools, we have access to greater resources and better practices. For example, we have directors of subjects, such as Maths, English, Performing Arts and Science, who move between the schools bringing the best practices and ensuring these are shared across us all. This is one of the most powerful things I have ever experienced, and ensures not only higher levels of consistency, but also higher levels of performance, confidence and accelerated development.

The headteacher then detailed the role of these directors, discussing the input they have on individual teachers, on the standardization of work and marking, and on the way they help raise the ambitions of departments by providing first-rate materials and concrete examples of how to use them. He concluded that teachers sharing within the profession is something that too many schools lack, and is one thing that everyone should always focus on, as it unites teams, develops individuals and improves performance.

Is this transformational leadership?

As was shown in Chapters 4 and 5, the evidence from the phase one research into headteacher leadership in challenging circumstances showed that transformational leaders focus on vision and communication, building and valuing relationships, motivating staff, empowering individuals, establishing self-belief and sharing leadership and are committed to the development of all members of the school community. Individuals are encouraged to take responsibility for their own actions and to be creative and innovative. The headteacher of Packwood School made references throughout to the vision for the school and his methods of communicating this with stakeholders.

Interviews with members of staff revealed that they also believed in, and carried, this same vision. One of the Heads of Department at Packwood viewed the school as:

> a place that is giving students the best education possible. Our aim is to get to outstanding, but we're not there yet; we are now on the right track to be an outstanding school, and therefore this is a place where students are achieving, and they are enjoying what they do. Results are going up. Students feel safe; they feel that teachers care about them.

The mention of aiming for the 'outstanding' Ofsted classification was used by other teachers whenever they were asked to describe the vision of the school; for some it was their first statement. One classroom teacher's vision was that they 'definitely want to strive to be an outstanding school'.

This ability of transformational leaders to share a vision for the school is accompanied by the idea that transformational leaders need to place great emphasis on building and valuing relationships. Evidence of this emphasis was revealed throughout the interviews, with one parent stating that the most significant change that had happened at the school was 'people respecting each other' and a member of the support staff adding that 'we all work together, as a team, and everyone is 100 percent behind each other'. Dr Hurst had described how important he believed it was that everyone felt supported and this feeling was one to which staff often referred; all those interviewed made positive references to support and recognized that there was a whole school approach where everyone did feel supported, both by other members of staff and the SLT.

Comments were also made by staff about the relationships that students had with each other and with members of staff. Every interviewee stated that students had much greater respect now for staff and for the other students in their lessons. One classroom Humanities teacher saw this as the greatest improvement in the school – one that could be seen in:

> the behaviour of the students in and around the academy; the way they get on with each other, the way that they get on with the staff. It's a lot calmer and a far more pleasant atmosphere...it enables me to teach my subject.

The improvement in student behaviour, therefore, is important in itself and also facilitates teaching more creatively and helps students to learn more effectively. Behavioural improvements also had a wider impact. Two lunchtime supervisors and 15 parents of students were interviewed about what had changed at Packwood, and they all suggested that the biggest change was that 'pupils are happier'. This was also noted by a Second in Science, who talked about the students' positive attitude; she recounted how the school had changed this year:

It's been pretty dramatic actually, the atmosphere in the school has changed generally; there are fewer pupils out in corridors and more pupils excited about getting to lessons. Pupils are just generally more positive about the school, overall there's a real buzz and excitement about learning and it's completely different to last year.

Another key feature of transformational leadership identified in the actions of the phase one study headteachers was the way in which leaders deploy motivation as a vehicle for achievement. The questionnaires completed for the implementation study by both parents and staff made references to the level of motivation being responsible for improvements within the school. One of the parents maintained that the biggest achievement had been 'enthusing teachers and hence students', making a direct link between the level of motivation in the school and the achievement of everyone involved. Similarly, responses to the staff questionnaires also mentioned the motivation of both staff and students. One respondent stated that the improvements had occurred because the 'behaviour and attitude in students has greatly improved and the motivation of staff has also improved'. According to another member of staff, the achievements had been made because of a more positive outlook by staff on pupils' outcomes and the higher expectations of students. Many staff made a direct reference to the motivation of students as being the greatest improvement in the school. One classroom teacher stated that the motivation of pupils, and the fact that they want to do well in lessons, was the one thing that was making all the difference. In agreement with this, a Second in MFL described how the motivation of students enabled everyone to take greater risks and achieve much more:

Pupils are motivated, they're engaged, and they're willing to try new things and take risks, which means we can take a lot more risks in lessons, so it is much more enjoyable. We get students who are motivated because they want to do well in that subject, and it's nice to teach them.

This is in full agreement with the idea that headteachers who are transformational focus on individuals, empowering them to achieve more, become flexible and develop a strong belief in their own abilities. A teacher of Spanish confirmed that his experiences in school were now completely different, as he was able to undertake much more in lessons than previously. He recounted how he had many ideas of activities that would improve learning, but had never dared try them because of how students behaved. Now he could confidently plan and deliver activities, secure in the knowledge that they would run smoothly and that students would gain the experiences he wanted them to. He went on to describe how unbelievable the change was, stating that it is the 'same kids but we can do so much more interesting and diverse activities; it's a very enjoyable atmosphere to teach in'. This empowering of teachers to deliver was also noted by students in their questionnaire responses, with some students making references to improvements in the quality of lessons and in the amount they achieve within lessons. Likewise, a governor who was also a member of the community stated in his questionnaire that it was the enhancements in the quality of teaching that had enabled the school to improve. Parents also agreed, with one stating that the improvement in the quality of teaching was the primary factor in her child's achievement and had resulted in her child enjoying being at school much more. Similarly, teachers also noted this, not only within their own lessons but throughout the school, with one teacher stating 'the standard of teaching here is now brilliant, just walking around the school you can see, in classrooms, fantastic lessons happening'. Many staff referred to this change as resulting from the support they now had from the school's senior leaders and the fact that they knew they were fully supported both in and out of the classroom; two members of staff stated in their interviews that they felt inspired to achieve more than ever before, and others added that they found this level of support to be very motivating.

It was argued in Chapters 4 and 5 that when leadership is transformational, not only does it alter the behaviours of others, but these changes start to mirror the behaviours of the leadership team and the head. Throughout the interviews at Packwood School, staff used words such as 'optimistic', 'inspiring', 'positive' and 'focused on achievement' to describe the leadership of the school. The same words were used when people were asked to sum up what the school was now like. This may indicate that the behaviour patterns of the leadership team are in fact being mirrored by others and are permeating aspects of school life, creating a school whose ethos is inseparable from the people who shape it. Throughout the interview with Dr Hurst, his responses could have been summed up using the same words, and it is possible that these could be used to describe his traits; it is feasible to draw a conclusion that these aspects of the school emanate from the head.

The study of the four headteachers in phase one of this research found that transformational headteachers are optimistic and excited about goals, and have a belief in the future and a commitment to develop and mentor others. Evidence of all of these characteristics emerged during the interview with the headteacher of Packwood School as he discussed not only his vision and belief of where the school could go, but also the goals he had for each department and how excited he was that they were well on the way to achieving these very challenging goals. Encouraging the development of others is said to be one of the main focuses of transformational leaders, and this was another aspect that was mirrored by staff within Packwood School. Heads of Department felt they were now developing the independence of staff within their departments, just as teachers felt they were developing the independence of students; one classroom Science teacher predicted that during the next 12 months 'the teaching in the classrooms is just going to get better and better...and pupils are becoming much more independent'.

The phase one research study found that headteachers are transformational when there is shared leadership and a shared empowerment, where a partnership is set up that includes aspects of coaching, mentoring and professional learning. This was a theme that also ran through the interviews and the questionnaires used for the implementation case study at Packwood School. One Head of Department discussed how the headteacher 'supported him in every way possible', which the Head of Department felt made all the difference in enabling him to perform his role. He also described how the headteacher's manner, which was always optimistic and creative, produced an environment where people felt they could achieve. Similarly, a Vice Principal stated that the school was now a great place to work, and accredited this to the headteacher enabling her to lead.

Dr Hurst stressed the importance he placed upon a consistent approach across the school, and stated that he felt that developing staff was key to achieving this. Interestingly, on the questionnaires returned from governors and staff, there were direct references to the level of consistency and how this was one of the leading factors that was generating improvements. Student questionnaires also made indirect references to this level of consistency, stating that lessons were now better, behaviour was dealt with in a better manner and that overall the general environment was better. The headteacher also described how he coached a group of school leaders, who could then generate a greater level of consistency; he stressed how pleased he was that they had started to develop on their own, without the need for continued direction from the headteacher. This reflects another aspect known to emerge through transformational leadership, that when leadership is transformational individuals take responsibility for their own actions and want to make a difference; indeed a further finding on transformational leaders is that they are more likely to be successful if they stimulate the creativity in followers than if they try to be the source of the creativity for a group of employees. The headteacher had drawn attention to examples of this, with the development of the 'wild-card' system and the greater involvement of students in the life of the school.

Students themselves felt they had been given more scope to be creative and had jointly led on a range of high-profile events throughout the school, including launching the school's Olympics Day and organizing a Jubilee celebration. In addition to this, the students felt they had made significant improvements to the running of the school, quoting changes to the school day as one of their major inputs, creating a split break time that they felt made the canteen a more pleasant place. Students also contributed to supporting the changes in the school, as Dr Hurst acknowledged:

> Students now play a much greater role in the leadership of the school, with Student Voice a prominent feature of the school and at every SLT meeting. The students have implemented many changes, all of which have been given the full backing of the Senior Leadership Team and have happened quickly, providing a momentum where students know they play a role in shaping the development of the school. The school now feels like we are one team, all pulling in the same direction.

New staff also felt they had made a positive contribution to the school, with some delivering their best practices to other staff and sharing the benefit of their creative classroom ideas. One classroom teacher had initiated a weekly flyer to highlight the best practices throughout the school, and she claimed to be inundated with submissions from staff who had lots of creative ideas to share. Another teacher had created an on-line forum for teachers to discuss creative classroom ideas that they were using and how to implement the topics covered in staff-training sessions to maximize impact. All of these aspects point to the conclusion that the leadership within the school is transformational in nature.

A study undertaken by Verona and Young (2001) into transformational leadership within schools found that it significantly increased the examination pass rates achieved by students, while simultaneously improving the moral base of personal growth of individuals within schools. These points are noticeable in Packwood School, with students stating that they take more responsibility for their actions and have a greater understanding of the consequences resulting from them. There is also evidence that supports the findings of Albritton (1995) that transformational leaders are very person centred, often give pep-talks and constantly nurture optimism and enthusiasm throughout the organization, empowering subordinates. It can be argued that headteachers are transformational leaders if they are open and fair with high levels of integrity, and the leader has full faith in the behaviours of the subordinates, believing that they are constantly striving to become better and perform at a superior level, and that they are self-driven and self-motivated with the goals of the organization at the centre of what they do (Leithwood and Jantzi, 2009). This sentiment was encapsulated by one response written on the back of an anonymous parent questionnaire:

I must admit that we reluctantly sent [our child] to [Packwood School] last September, but it was the choice she made and because we'd had such a major upheaval in our lives, we wanted her to be happy. [Our child] has only been here a few months so the questions asked overleaf [about the changes that have taken place within the school] didn't apply so much to us. Admitting that, I can honestly say, so far we haven't regretted it. [Our child] is very happy here. In my opinion Dr Hurst, his SLT and the vast majority of his staff are fully committed to getting back on track, and are succeeding.

Conclusions: From kicked-in doors to a 'welcoming, friendly learning environment'

Dr Hurst's general view was that although there is still some way to go, Packwood School is now a place of learning where students and staff felt safe and were focused on achieving. He described it as a 'calm, peaceful place of learning' and cited many examples of evidence that students and staff were now committed to the process of learning. These included the manner in which students purposefully moved to lessons on the warning bell, without the need for anyone to instruct them, and the fact that there had not been a single fire alarm set off maliciously, or that there were no corridor doors kicked off their hinges; indeed, he claimed that the deliberate damage bill had fallen by tens of thousands of pounds. He stated that an even greater indication of the focus on learning was the way that students actively sought out their teachers now, to hand in homework early or to share details of something they have achieved. He continued to describe how the quality of what was happening in the classrooms was unrecognizable after the changes, and how many visitors had told him this. Dr Hurst spoke of how when he now walked around the school he could see teachers enjoying teaching and students enjoying learning:

I often show visitors around the lessons, and they are always amazed. I make the promise that we will go into any lesson at any time, and they will not see any misbehaviour of any type, or a child off task. Last week I showed some members of the local authority around, who had previously visited the school. As we walked from exciting lesson to exciting lesson, one of the members of the local authority told me what he saw had given him goosebumps. The other told me it was amazing how students enter and leave the dining hall without the need for supervision any more. Behaviour is now exemplary and students are receiving full hour lessons of learning instead of 10 minutes of learning and 50 minutes of putting up with disruption. Teachers are trying new strategies and taking greater risks; they now state that they can teach again and love it. As a consequence, achievement is increasing and students are starting to take pride in themselves and their accomplishments. Everyone who visits the school states that it is like being in a completely different place; the ethos; the attitudes and the enjoyment are all unrecognizable.

This is Dr Hurst's account of the ways in which a school that has always struggled to perform and has been classed as being in challenging circumstances for a considerable amount of time can be, and has been, improved. His account made direct and deliberate references to transformational leadership, stating that he had consciously made a decision to follow this route. Evidence collected from other staff, from governors, students and parents appeared to validate these claims and provided evidence that the school was being led in a style that could be mapped onto signposts of transformational leadership. More importantly, this model was generating dramatic and quick improvements, as can be seen by all the measures used. By considering a range of different criteria, it is possible to draw parallels between the practical leadership of the school and the theoretical model of transformational leadership, indicating that this model could be responsible for the changes that had taken place.

The headteacher stressed his view that becoming an academy was not responsible for the improvements; in fact he felt that some other academy chains did not generate improvements at all. Instead, it was the transformational nature by which this particular chain operates that was responsible for generating the improvements, and this could have been achieved without adopting academy status, but by simply aligning with the successful organizations involved and by the deployment of appropriate forms of leadership and support. For Dr Hurst, it was the factors that were more influential, namely those of sharing best practice, coaching and developing staff, and building confidence and self-belief. Finally, the question as to whether this style of leadership can bring about rapid changes, build self-confidence in others and provide greater opportunities is addressed by considering a letter of thanks given to the headteacher by a student. This particular letter was from a student who had been part of the school's Student Voice team, and after leaving the school, had returned to pass on his thanks:

Dear Dr Hurst and the Senior Leadership Team,

I would just like to take this opportunity to thank you for everything you and your team have done for me this year. I cannot tell you how much it means to me to have been able to be a part of the significant changes that have transformed [Packwood School] this year!

I now leave [Packwood School], a totally different place from this time last year. The work you have undertaken is truly unbelievable. But I believe all the hard work and effort has been really worthwhile. [Packwood School] is now a welcoming, friendly learning environment and the ethos of the whole school, students and teachers alike, is one that many other schools could never hope to re-create.

I honestly believe that without your leadership at [Packwood School], a great number of Year 11s would have been failed by the school. So, thanks for your positive and determined attitude towards wanting change to take place and for being a figurehead for that transformation – I now see a fantastic place for learning and a setting to be proud. I am now jealous as my younger sister will be here for the next five years to enjoy it and of course reap the benefits.

I strongly believe that now there is a real sense of achievement and recognition of success at [Packwood School]. I have been so lucky to have been here for just one year…I wish for everyone at the school to embrace the changes and adopt the new attitude towards learning and it will continue to be a truly inspiring place to learn for many years into the future.

On a personal note, I will never be able to thank you enough for giving me the opportunity to be Vice-President. The important lessons I have learnt through this experience I shall take with me for the rest of my life; the knowledge, the self-confidence, the social skills. I know that the Student Voice will grow and grow – this is down to the belief you have in the students here at [Packwood School].

You have been a real inspiration.

A massive THANK YOU!

(Letter handed in to the school in June 2012)

7

Successful Leadership in Challenging Circumstances: From Theory to Implementation

The first phase of this extended, two-phase research study had two key aims. The first was to explore the extent to which headteachers working within a local authority in challenging circumstances reported that they deployed transactional and transformational leadership. The second was to identify where and when the headteachers deployed transformational leadership and to establish what strategies they would use to do this. Data identifying the heads' leadership style and the factors affecting their choice of approaches to leadership were collected during semi-structured interviews with both the headteachers and their deputies. The analysis was conducted within a theoretical framework derived from transactional and transformational leadership theory and linked to the constructivist paradigm, which explores the relationship between values and leadership action. This theoretical framework made it possible both to examine the approaches to leadership adopted by the headteachers at a conceptual level and to explore in detail the leadership choices they made and the factors which either facilitated or constrained their choices.

The local authority in the main study, Coalborough, is situated in northern England in a former mining area with high levels of deprivation. This is reflected in the schools by low attendance rates, concerns about behaviour and difficulties in recruiting teachers. The local authority has found it difficult to make any significant, lasting improvements to schools, and several were placed in special measures in the four years prior to the study. Others were issued with a notice to improve from Ofsted and managed to meet the benchmark targets within a year of receiving the notice, preventing their being placed in special measures. One of the schools in this study, Blackwood, has been placed in special measures twice, which spurred the local authority to seek support from another authority where many of the schools are judged to be 'good' or better. Blackwood School's leadership was replaced, since when all the schools in this sample have been considered to be led by successful headteachers.

The Coalborough study placed great emphasis on the headteachers' self-reported styles, in the belief that headteachers have a strong understanding of the actions they take and their implications (Southworth, 1995). Deputies from each school were also interviewed to provide a means of verifying and testing statements made by the headteachers. Statistical and inspection data, including examination grade trends and the most recent Ofsted reports, were used to provide context for the schools. The schools in the main sample were all secondary, comprehensive schools with Specialist Status. Three of the schools have a sixth form but the highest achieving school, Raleigh, does not. Greville School is slightly smaller than average as measured by the number of students on roll, but the other three schools are all larger than an average comprehensive school. The catchments for all schools are broadly similar, with Raleigh School having slightly higher-than-average achieving students on entry, and the others having lower than average, with Greville School having the lowest-achieving students on entry. The schools' characteristics mean they represent a good spread of the schools within the authority and, while not being statistically representative, can be said to be typical examples.

The headteachers in this study came to their present schools in different ways. Blackwood School is led by a headteacher and deputy who were seconded from a secondary school in a different authority, neither of whom had held a position at this level before. The head of Greville School was formerly its deputy and accepted the headship when his predecessor retired seven years ago. The other two headteachers have been heads in different authorities and have served as headteachers in this authority for over ten years. The head of Yarborough School was asked by the local authority to take over the leadership of a second, failing, school within the same authority at the start of this academic year. Although it is difficult to make a judgement on the ability of the headteachers, due to the complexities involved in leadership, the assumption that these headteachers are successful was made following their most recent Ofsted reports, where each school was given a grading of 'good'. In addition to this, none of the schools led by these headteachers has ever been placed in special measures, or given a notice to improve by Ofsted. Exercises to measure the standards of schools are carried out by external organizations using existing criteria set by governmental agencies. On this basis, therefore, these schools are judged to be successful and to have good leadership. Every deputy had worked with their headteacher for more than five years and, with the exception of Blackwood School, had all served in their current school for at least this time. The accounts of deputy headteachers are considered reliable additional means of exploration in this study because deputies often work closely with the headteacher and may have additional insights to offer.

The school in the implementation case study, Packwood, is similar to the schools in the main study except for being part of an academy group of schools. The local authority where it is situated, Willbridge, is considerably larger than Coalborough. It has 47 secondary schools and covers a much larger area with a more diverse spread of achievements. Unemployment is broadly in line with the national average, but this masks significant disparities. Packwood School is situated in a former mining area where every secondary school has been categorized by Ofsted as underperforming. Packwood, however, was the only one placed into special measures. The school was created in 2004 when two underachieving schools were merged, and it was hoped that the better of the two schools, which itself had been categorized as having serious weaknesses by Ofsted, would help lift the other school out of special measures. Instead, the new merged school was classified by Ofsted as inadequate and placed in special measures before the current head, Dr Hurst, was appointed. He was the third person to hold the Packwood headship since 2004, and had been involved in the main Coalborough research study when he was a deputy headteacher.

The initial study took as its starting point existing definitions of transactional and transformational leadership (Albritton, 1995; Drago-Severson, 2002; Eagly et al., 2003) to provide an analytical framework for the leadership actions of headteachers. Both transactional and transformational leadership theories place the headteacher at the heart of school developments, due to the way in which these theories allow leaders to exercise their power base. Transactional leadership focuses on fostering the notion of transactions taking place between the follower and the leader, whereas transformational leadership focuses on the leader inspiring and motivating followers, fostering within them a desire to improve and achieve. Headteachers were most transformational when they were person-centred, concentrating on the development of individuals rather than being concerned with results or outcomes. This study was based on the generally accepted assumption that the work of the headteacher is the most influential aspect of a school's success or failure. The participating heads certainly took this view. Based on the argument advanced by Bottery (2004) and Liebman et al., (2005) the heads also accepted that headteachers can have a greater effect on the daily practices of people within schools by adopting transactional and transformational approaches. A similar stance was adopted in the implementation case study, where the head of Packwood School, Dr Hurst, was certainly central to the changes which took place. In this case, however, Dr Hurst had access to the findings of the main study, having been a deputy in one of the schools involved, and was able to adopt a series of transformational strategies derived from that study.

Transactional leadership: Demonstrating high standards

Eagly *et al.*, (2003), Davies (2007) and Northouse (2007) point out the benefits of both transactional and transformational leadership to the work of headteachers. Murugan (2004) and Cameron (2006) argue that headteachers adopt a transactional approach to undertake managerial duties due to the simplified manner in which progress can be tracked and measured. When the actions of the Coalborough headteachers in the phase one study were analysed, mapped onto instances of transactional leadership and grouped in order of frequency, it was clear that the headteachers adopted a transactional approach most often when concentrating on the completion of tasks and ensuring the maintaining of high standards. External pressures placed on the headteachers within this study were found to be linked very strongly with the decision of headteachers to adopt a transactional approach to leadership, so these headteachers adopted this role of transactional leader in order to embed policies, identify and deal with underperformance or respond to Ofsted inspections. The mechanistic approach to leadership under a transactional style provides headteachers with a rigid set of tracking criteria against which they can measure progress following intervention. These headteachers favoured this method when justifying their actions to government agencies due to the level of rigidity and simplified methods of measuring success. The implication of these findings is that headteachers are pushed towards the less developmental style of transactional leadership wherever they lose autonomy or are held accountable by external, political pressures. In schools situated in challenging circumstances, the community is very susceptible to political changes. Schools need to adapt quickly, and feel they are constantly under scrutiny from external agencies to ensure that schools meet benchmarked targets. In these circumstances, the desire to be graded 'good' by Ofsted becomes even more essential. It takes self-confidence born of experience to cope with such pressures.

Perhaps this explains why the least experienced headteacher (the head of Blackwood School) tended to use transactional rather than transformational leadership, whilst believing that she was transformational in her approach.

This was demonstrated when she identified her reluctance to deviate from the 'vision' of a school structure which she had brought over from her previous school. The vision was obviously not conceptualized in the future, as she already had concrete evidence of how this structure worked. This approach can possibly be explained by her inexperience of running a school and her belief that, since the model worked in the previous school, it would also work in her current post. Similarly, there was evidence that the other headteachers in the sample had been more transactional when they were new to the post. The implications are that either new headteachers attempt to implement a familiar, successful model into different surroundings, without allowances being made for different skills, personalities or resources, or that less experienced heads focus on tested, measurable (and therefore transactional) actions, not having developed confidence in their own vision and in their own and others' capabilities.

In the implementation case study, Dr Hurst used both transactional and transformational leadership, although he was able to minimize the adverse effects of deploying transactional leadership. He was able to limit the extent to which it was used and to turn many instances of transactional leadership into transformational opportunities by focusing on personal and professional development, thus using transactional leadership to facilitate transformations within Packwood School. Even the rigorous application of school rules on student behaviour and almost formulaic approaches to pedagogy provided such opportunities. Dr Hurst also benefited from being able to deploy leadership strategies derived from the main study. Nevertheless, like the head of Blackwood School in the main study, Dr Hurst's frequent references to Ofsted and to external examination criteria demonstrate the impact that external criteria can have on the leadership within a school. The difference at Packwood School seems to be that Dr Hurst had access to a different model of leadership that could be readily adapted to the circumstances of his school.

Transformational leadership: Creating high standards

When the headteachers in the phase one study behaved in a transformational manner, they were extremely vision driven, acting as change agents with the intention of bringing about long-term, sustainable improvements to their school, or even to their community. They placed great emphasis on their core values and on the collaboration and involvement of others in the creation and achievement of an inspirational vision. The context of the schools and their communities is a major factor in determining the leadership style of the headteachers. Serving in socially deprived areas, the headteachers expressed desires to raise aspirations above all else. They often referred to their values of wanting equality and fairness for all. In the phase one study the data was explored further to examine how far the headteachers regarded themselves as transformational leaders and the importance they attached to values, communication, motivation and building relationships within the school and in the wider community.

This study also found that the four headteachers tended to become more transformational over time. This may, in part, be explained by an analysis based on the constructivist paradigm, which suggests that, due to the enhanced feedback headteachers receive when serving in a socially deprived area, there is a close link between the values headteachers espouse and their perceptions of reality in challenging circumstances. In a socially deprived area the actions of headteachers seem to have a greater impact and produce faster feedback, which in turn reinforces the belief of the headteacher that they are able to make significant improvements to transform their community. This belief in their ability to bring about positive change in turn affects the headteachers' actions and thoughts, moving them towards a reality where they do indeed make greater, significant changes by becoming a transformational leader. The positive feedback from changes and the resulting desire to make greater changes produce a loop that moves headteachers towards transformational leadership.

The implications for schools can be significant: the performance and ability of staff are improved, raising the standards of schools in socially deprived areas. Successful headteachers tend to adopt transformational leadership as a means of increasing the flexibility to maximize the resources at their disposal, while bringing about sustainable improvements and igniting the belief in people that they can achieve and that they have the same potential as others. It was noted that the heads in the main study went beyond the expected level of transformational leaders and became more passionate about wanting to help members of the wider community who, they felt, existed in social and economic poverty. These heads had a genuine concern for individuals, including those who had already left the school and those who were not even associated with the school. It is possible that the positive feedback from serving a deprived community generates a stronger desire in headteachers to continue to serve, and provides the purpose needed for headteachers in challenging circumstances to persevere and succeed. It was also evident in the implementation case study that Dr Hurst and his staff valued positive responses from members of the wider community within which Packwood School is situated. It was also evident, however, that the focus at Packwood School is, and perhaps has to be, on improving the overall performance of teachers and students within the school even if this generates some critical responses from the wider community.

In both the Coalborough study and in the Packwood School case study, the preferred leadership style and the detailed strategies deployed by the headteachers were influenced by the school context, as well as by professional experience. The longer-term sustainable development of a school in challenging circumstances requires leadership that is embedded in a culture focused on clear values and the educational success of all, and is voiced in a vision that is carried by staff, students and members of the community. This lends itself to a transformational approach, as the changes that result are embedded into the fabric of the workforce and generate sustainable improvements. When a headteacher is concerned about whole-school improvement, that concern can create deep changes in culture and ethos, and they utilize the skills associated with transformational leaders. When striving for long-lasting changes, whether in the context of a school or of an entire community, it is through transformational leadership that the future vision is embraced, and that more members become involved. Transformational leaders are able to influence more people due to their ability to inspire others and lead by example. Their foundation for leadership is based on their own values, which drive them through adversity and lead to greater achievements for all.

Although these values may differ somewhat between headteachers, and be expressed in different ways in each school, the Coalborough research study showed that the successful headteachers in this study of leaders in challenging circumstances adopted both transactional and transformational approaches to leadership, depending partly on the circumstances and partly on their experience as headteachers but, more importantly, also on their values and the ways in which those values are translated into a vision for the school. While each of these approaches to leadership tended to be used by the headteachers for different purposes, there is no doubt that the headteachers favoured transformational leadership based on participation, collaboration and a commitment to supporting their staff and facilitating professional development wherever possible. This approach to transformational leadership was grounded in a strong value system, a clear sense of purpose and a strong commitment to the local community, and enabled these headteachers to cope with both the educational and social challenges that they encountered on a daily basis and to be successful by having the capacity to translate these values and beliefs into actions.

Finding a transformational leadership style

It has been seen that, in contrast to the external, political pressures that encouraged the headteachers to become transactional, it was internal measures that encouraged headteachers' leadership style to become transformational. It was also noted that where headteachers were transformational, they articulated a desire to see others succeed and improve – not only to achieve targets for the school but for their own well-being. In the Coalborough study, the headteachers' wish to see others succeed was not limited to the students or staff, but extended to school-leavers and even members of the community not directly associated with the school. In the implementation case study support was provided for those staff who wanted to leave the school as well as for the remaining staff and students, illustrating the extent to which headteachers operated at a high level of value-based leadership. The headteachers' reliance upon their own values was evident throughout both studies. These values, they believed, provided a foundation that underpinned all their actions. These included the right for everyone to be treated with respect and to be given every opportunity to succeed, irrespective of their background or starting position within the school. It was clear, especially at Packwood School, that this applied even to the most difficult of students. Although these values were fixed, the headteachers also revealed instances of how they constantly checked their values and questioned the paradigm within which they acted, especially when dealing with unexpected events. Thus, the headteachers' use of transformational leadership was an emergent theme for success and was linked to their actions, as dictated by their core values.

The Coalborough research study provided evidence that, in schools in challenging circumstances, headteachers prefer a transformational approach due to their perceived need to bring about major changes, and due to the values of headteachers ensuring they provide equality in a deprived area. Although many other studies (Anderson and Anderson, 2001; Hybels, 2002) reveal that transformational leadership is considered the most appropriate route for bringing about successful changes, they do not investigate either the centrality of values to such processes or the level of desire on the part of headteachers to want these changes, especially when situated in an area where they feel social justice is lacking. Lambert (2009), however, in her analysis of constructivist leadership, provides examples of how the perception of inequality is a higher-level value that can produce outrage in value-driven individuals, directing them to find solutions to address any equality discrepancies. She does not, though, link this with the process of finding solutions through transformational leadership. Leithwood and Jantzi (2009) and Harris and Thompson (2006) recognize the importance of headteacher leadership, as does Rhode (2006) when she examines moral leadership, although leadership is not conceptualized as transformational in these studies. Harris and Chapman (2002) note that effective leaders in schools facing challenging circumstances:

> offer leadership that is value-driven with a strong moral purpose. They are deeply concerned about the welfare and the educational experiences of all pupils in their care.

> (HARRIS AND CHAPMAN, 2002: 3)

Headteachers serving in challenging circumstances believed that their key role was to bring about change in order to alter the perceptions that students, staff and the community have about schools. This focus on change meant that the heads felt the need to relay their values and vision constantly, encouraging others to act as change agents and to play a role in improving the community, which resulted in their adopting a transformational approach. In so doing, these headteachers used transformational leadership to influence the beliefs of others and shape the communities which they served. Headteachers gravitate towards transformational leadership whenever possible and accredit instances of this as being responsible for their successes, although the heads understood that they could not necessarily bring about the required changes alone and that they needed active collaboration from colleagues.

The increased possibility of extended collaboration with colleagues inside the school and with members of the wider community allows them to implement new ideas while, at the same time, developing individuals within their schools. This is of vital importance when headteachers are required to lead through the uncertainty associated with the changing nature of education, especially in socially deprived areas where political changes can have severe effects on the community. Such a level of uncertainty requires that headteachers be more flexible and able to meet the real-world requirements of constantly changing systems, and encourages them to move away from the fixed nature of transactional leadership and towards the fluid, evolving nature of transformational leadership.

To facilitate collaboration colleagues need to be highly motivated. In both the main study and in the implementation study, headteachers revealed their belief in motivation as a vehicle for achievement and approached this almost as tacit knowledge, which was factual and implicit. Deputy headteachers, heads of department and teachers were encouraged and motivated, enabling them to push forward with change and make creative breakthroughs, helping to foster improvements in education and further developments in the capabilities of everyone within the school. Every headteacher placed great importance on the transformational characteristics of raising aspirations and changing the self-beliefs of others. They discussed the motivational aspects of their role as if they were not optional but fundamental and absolute, implying that they could not perform without the ability to inspire their followers. Similarly, headteachers constantly questioned their own beliefs and reflected on their own practices. They tended to be learners who developed over time. They had the opportunity to grow and develop alongside the staff, resulting in schools that were constantly improving and developing greater capacity, and were able to adapt to meet the needs of individuals, while simultaneously aligning with new political agendas.

The constructivist paradigm and transformational leadership: A symbiotic relationship

Lambert (2009) notes the importance of continued professional development when she considers the constructivist learner. She argues that new experiences and new information are assimilated by looking for patterns and constructing meanings from them. These newly constructed meanings then alter all future actions. The two research studies considered here take Lambert's work further by considering the marriage between the constructivist paradigm and the headteacher's view of reality in challenging circumstances. As already demonstrated, the positive feedback that arises from changes and the consequent desire to make greater changes are interdependent and move headteachers towards a transformational leadership style. As the head of Blackwood School pointed out when discussing her students, her entire belief system was centred on ensuring students were always placed first and that there was mutual respect between staff and students. She demonstrated a similar view when she described her belief in her Senior Leadership Team (SLT), which she described as very skilled, effective and completely trustworthy in every sense. The head of Packwood School took a similar position on both students and his SLT. At Packwood School, the ethos of the school might be summed up by the phrases 'students first' and 'the school is run for the students, not the staff'. This approach shaped the nature of the changes that were introduced in this failing school, from rules about uniform and behaviour to guidelines on lesson planning, pedagogy and the structure of option choices. The SLT was required to shift its focus from administration to supporting teaching, learning and improving discipline in the school, and to contribute to staff training and development at the individual teacher level, through coaching, and at departmental and school levels through contributing to formal and informal training and development programmes. The head of Yarborough School considered that schools need headteachers who are strategic thinkers and can solve problems. By seeking out problems to solve, this headteacher is able to create a reality where, as a successful headteacher, he is able to remove obstacles and find creative solutions. Such problem-solving must be grounded in strong relationships. The head of Greville School explained that in his view relationships are the one key feature that is critical to a school's success; he considered his relationship with staff and students to be very positive. This had been a priority for him, taking action to ensure good relationships were formed. He then accredited the success of the school to the developments they had made in forming these stronger relationships.

These views indicate that the success achieved by the headteachers might be attributed to transformational leadership based on person-centred actions, communications and outcomes. Hence, headteachers not only demonstrated an awareness that they could instigate change, but also were confident that they could make significant changes. This strong belief in people could in some way help to identify and explain their success. There was, however, some evidence to suggest that this is a characteristic that appears to develop over time and that headteachers evolve with the schools they are leading. Thus, in an environment where there is large-scale deprivation, the headteachers studied believed they were successful if they could raise aspirations and motivate followers towards improvement. To achieve this, the headteachers acted as transformational leaders to the extent that they recognized the importance of developing the whole individual. This then enabled the headteachers to create a development cycle of improvement and of wanting to create more improvements for pupils, colleagues and members of the wider community.

Strategies for transformational leadership

At Packwood School recognizing the importance of both staff and students was at the core of all the strategies that Dr Hurst introduced; this was comparable to the schools in the Coalborough study. These strategies, which are summarized in Table 7.1, had to be introduced in parallel rather than piecemeal in order to address the significant difficulties that confronted Dr Hurst and his staff. Gradual change was simply not an option. It was necessary to address issues relating to the school culture and its underpinning values, pupil behaviour, pedagogy and assessment, restoring and improving staff morale and personal and professional development at all levels in the school. Consequently, many of the strategies deployed were intended to target several aspects of the work of Packwood School at one and the same time.

The case study of Packwood School shows the importance of a fresh start for any school in challenging circumstances with a new headteacher. At Packwood, the vision for the school was based on putting students first and emphasizing that all students deserved an equal chance to benefit from a good education. This was the starting point for change. It did not mean, however, that unacceptable behaviour, lateness for lessons and vandalism would be tolerated. The reverse was the case. By strictly enforcing a set of clear and simple rules, Dr Hurst and his colleagues were able to ensure that all students benefited. The same was true for the teaching staff. A set of guidelines for lesson planning and delivery, marking and assessment, departmental organization and restructuring parts of the curriculum were supported by training, coaching and mentoring of all staff. The role of the

TABLE 7.1 Strategies for leading schools in challenging circumstances – based on Packwood School

Strategic focus	Examples	Intention
Change the culture and start afresh.	Forget reasons for previous failures. All students start with a clean slate.	Focus on the future not on the past.
Establish and share a simple vision in a few key words.	Students first.	Must shape every part of school life.
Head must lead by example.	Teaching students and providing training for colleagues.	Heads must be seen to practice what they preach.
SLT must set example.	Focus on core strategic tasks.	SLT must be seen to be supporting staff in all aspects of work.
Build and value relationships.	Work with individuals and small groups. Meet requests for support.	Establish and develop trust and confidence throughout the whole staff team.
Leadership must be shared and staff must be empowered.	Establish ways of ensuring that all staff and students have a role in making decisions.	The voices of staff and students must he heard at school and departmental level.
Everything must connect to purpose.	Establish an agreed model for teaching and assessment. More responsive option structures.	Every part of teaching and learning must be purposeful and meet student needs. School and departmental performance targets must be met.
Establish and enforce clear rules.	Uniform. Classroom behaviour.	No exceptions and no backing down.

(continued)

Strategic focus	Examples	Intention
Invest heavily in people.	Provide staff training, coaching and mentoring.	Head and SLT must give their time to supporting colleagues.
Develop staff capacity.	Encourage staff to share good practice with colleagues.	All working practices including teaching and administration must be improved.
Foster creativity.	Encourage staff to experiment and develop new ways to teaching to foster improved learning.	Move beyond established practice but attach no blame to failure.
Take individual responsibility.	Encourage staff to take initiatives such as 'wild cards'.	Help all staff to improve their own practice and to share this with others.
Provide constant challenges.	Help staff to find ways of continuously improving.	The school must keep moving forward and staff must be flexible and responsive to the need to change.

SLT was changed to ensure that the work of senior leaders had a strategic focus, rather than allowing them to concern themselves with the minutiae of school life. They had to be seen about the school, supporting and encouraging colleagues. By helping to identify good practice and innovative teaching, the SLT contributed to the improvement of teaching and learning and to fostering creativity. This, in turn, was supported by training, coaching and mentoring. All staff were encouraged to play a part in decision making and in sharing good practice. In the face of the constant need to improve and move the school forward, teachers both needed this help in developing their own capacity and provided ways of developing the capacity of others.

Conclusion: Misquoting the Beatles

The concept of the relationship between input and outcome was expressed, if not discovered, by McCartney (1969). The two linked research studies into school leadership in challenging circumstances could therefore be summarized by echoing the Beatles' aphorism: 'And in the end, the change you make is equal to the leadership you create' (with apologies to McCartney, 1969). The challenging circumstances in which the four heads in the phase one study, and Dr Hurst in the implementation case study, operate are a significant part of the context which helps to determine the leadership styles that they adopt. Transactional and transformational leadership are both deployed in these schools, but for different purposes. Transactional leadership is implemented for task-orientated actions and, although it does not develop a school, it may be necessary to underpin its smooth running, especially when meeting targets set by national policies and external organizations. This is vital in local authorities such as those in these two studies, where underperformance of schools is a constant concern. There is not, however, a distinct dichotomy between transactional and transformational interactions; as Dr Hurst shows, the former can be used in a transformative way while still achieving the accountability for which transactional interactions are often used. However, it is worth noting that systems with better educational outcomes often have considerably less demanding forms of accountability than those which, in England, produce an emphasis on transactional leadership (Glatter, 2012).

Transactional leadership may provide the groundwork to move the school forward, as it will ensure that the school is viewed as successful when subjected to external measurement criteria, providing greater freedom for the headteacher than does a school that is viewed as failing. Education policy requires educational organizations to increase pupil participation and standards, as well as to have the ability to provide guidance and support during difficult social times (Stevenson, 2006). This is tied to the funding received by headteachers; often the funding needed to achieve it is considered to be insufficient, resulting in an imbalance between expected increases in performance and the level of resources available (Whitfield, 2000). In order to be successful in today's climate, headteachers must excel in all areas if they are to meet government agendas. Transactional leadership alone cannot secure this level of performance, especially when funding is insufficient to be able to create a financial motivation for staff. These two linked pieces of research have shown that higher levels of success can be achieved by embedding transformational leadership in development plans for leaders at all levels within schools in order to increase motivation and staff development, providing a workforce which is both inspirational and aspirational. Successful headteachers are transformational but, in a socially deprived area, they go beyond the expected level of transformational leadership to become even more inspirational, with even more emphasis on altering the perceptions of others. They have a strong belief in people and see more in them than others do. Headteachers must have faith in their ability to shape the future of their schools, coupled with a positive outlook. This faith in the future must be shared in all the headteachers' communications, relaying their values with a strong focus on the idea that everyone can continue to improve at all levels. Such headteachers are inspirational, motivational and focused on developing individuals.

The two studies have shown that these headteachers in schools in challenging circumstances all deployed both transactional and transformational leadership. However, it is clear that transactional leadership tends to be utilized largely because the headteachers are required to respond to targets and other outside pressures, mainly of a mechanistic or managerial nature, which forces them to focus on immediate results and detailed supervision of staff performance. Headteachers in this study have argued that such transactional leadership contributes little of value to the overall development and success of their schools, while, at the same time, limiting the extent to which they can act autonomously and be guided by their own ethical values. It is the transformational leadership activities that largely facilitate long-term improvements in pupil attainment and the development of staff, and that strengthen valuable links with the wider community. Each of these headteachers made it clear that transformational leadership, firmly grounded in a clear set of values and beliefs that inform their approach to headship, was their preferred approach to the leadership of their schools. They highlighted the particular importance of these values in the challenging contexts within which they work and identified the key role that transformational leadership plays in their success. It could be argued, therefore, that a reduction in the externally imposed accountability and reporting requirements that produce an emphasis on transactional leadership might enable headteachers to concentrate their attention on the more important – and more effective – transformational activities. It is possible that the additional resources thus created would facilitate a greater degree of transformational activity and result in a greater beneficial impact on the school, students and local communities in challenging circumstances.

Appendix 1

Statistical data for all schools within Coalborough local authority for the academic year 2007–2008

School name	Percentage of students achieving equivalent to five GCSEs at grades A* to C including English and Maths	Contextual Value Added Score from KS2 to KS4
School name removed	66	1015.1
School name removed	66	993.2
Raleigh School	60	1008.8
School name removed	56	1004.6
School name removed	50	1002.1
School name removed	40	1002.9
School name removed	37	1025
School name removed	37	988.8
Blackwood School	35	981.3
Greville School	30	1010.7
School name removed	30	983.8
School name removed	29	980.8

(continued)

School name	Percentage of students achieving equivalent to five GCSEs at grades A* to C including English and Maths	Contextual Value Added Score from KS2 to KS4
Yarborough School	28	981.5
School name removed	26	1010.6
School name removed	24	980.1
School name removed	21	971.9
School name removed	19	976.4

Source: http://www.education.gov.uk (2008)

Appendix 2

GCSE results for Packwood School analysed by student category and date

Five A* to C for different groups	2011	2012	Change
Boys (%)	67	87	Increased by 20
Girls (%)	77	95	Increased by 18
Special educational needs (school action) (%)	39	78	Increased by 39
Special educational needs (school action plus) (%)	14	63	Increased by 49
Special educational needs (statemented) (%)	n/a	100	
Free school meals (%)	45	81	Increased by 36
Vulnerable (looked after children) (%)	40	100	Increased by 60

Five A* to C including English and Maths for different groups	2011	2012	Change
Boys (%)	38	53	Increased by 15
Girls (%)	44	61	Increased by 17

(continued)

Five A* to C including English and Maths for different groups	2011	2012	Change
Special educational needs (school action) (%)	6	18	Increased by 12
Special educational needs (school action plus) (%)	0	13	Increased by 13
Special educational needs (statemented) (%)	n/a	0	
Free school meals (%)	10	26	Increased by 16
Vulnerable (looked after children) (%)	40	100	Increased by 60

Five A* to C including English and Maths and Science for different groups	2011	2012	Change
Boys (%)	28	48	Increased by 20
Girls (%)	40	58	Increased by 18
Special educational needs (school action) (%)	2	18	Increased by 16
Special educational needs (school action plus) (%)	0	0	
Special educational needs (statemented) (%)	n/a	0	
Free school meals (%)	6	21	Increased by 15
Vulnerable (looked after children) (%)	20	100	Increased by 80

Evidence of sustainability and continual improvement

Fifty-three percent of 2012 Year 10 students enter Year 11 with an A* to C in Maths (compared with 17 percent in 2011). In 2012, the current Year 10 students already achieved more A* grades in Maths than the current Year 11 finished with.

In 2012, 31 percent of Year 10 students had already achieved a grade A* to C in French, compared with Year 11, who left with 20 percent of the cohort achieving an A* to C grade in French.

In 2012, 99.3 percent of Year 10 students already had at least one GCSE at a grade C or above before they started Year 11, compared with Year 11, who finished with 98.5 percent of the cohort achieving one A* to C.

In March 2013, the new Year 11 students received results from early entries in English and Maths. At this time, they already have 68 percent in English and 73 percent in Maths, with several months left before the end-of-year exams. It can be seen that these results are already above the record-breaking results achieved in September 2012.

Appendix 3

Comparison of GCSE grades achieved by Packwood School in 2011 and 2012

GCSE Subjects	2011	2012	Change
5 A* to C including E&M **(FFTD Target = 52%)** (%)	41	57	Increased by 16
5 A* to C **(FFTD Target = 79%)** (%)	72	91	Increased by 19
5 A* to G (%)	89	96	Increased by 7
1 A* to C (%)	87	99	Increased by 12
1 A* to G (%)	96	100	Increased by 4
5 A* to A (%)	16	19	Increased by 3
5 A* to C including English, Maths and Science (%)	33	53	Increased by 20
English A* to C **(FFTD Target = 63%)** (%)	47	64	Increased by 17
Maths A* to C **(FFTD Target = 57%)** (%)	52	65	Increased by 13
Also, 12 students passed AS-level Maths – including 4 grade As (%)			
Science 2 A* to Cs	53	81	Increased by 28
Art (applied 2 GCSE equivalent) (%)	96	100	Increased by 4
Art GCSE (%)	71	71	
Business studies GCSE (%)	31	91	Increased by 60
Business studies diploma (4 GCSE equivalent) (%)	96	100	Increased by 4

(continued)

GCSE Subjects	2011	2012	Change
Child development (%)	49	71	Increased by 22
Citizenship (%)	62	92	Increased by 30
Design technology (electronics) (%)	12	73	Increased by 61
Design technology (product design) (%)	New	93	
Design technology (resistant materials) (%)	33	47	Increased by 14
Design technology (textiles) (%)	New	75	
Drama (%)	69	54	Fell by 15
French (%)	75	95	Increased by 20
Geography (%)	58	69	Increased by 11
Hair (city and guilds 3 GCSEs at grade B) (%)	New	83	Increased by 20
History (%)	61	81	Increased by 8
Hospitality and catering (%)	86	94	
ICT national award (2 GCSEs) (%)	100	100	
ICT certificate (3 GCSEs) (%)	100	100	
Media studies (2 GCSEs) (%)	100	100	
Motor vehicle engineering (%)	New	53	
Music (%)	71	91	Increased by 20
PE GCSE (%)	49	87	Increased by 38
Public services (%)	92	100	Increased by 8
Religious education (%)	34	100	Increased by 66
Number of A* grades	21	41	Improved by 20
Number of U grades	73	15	Improved by 58
3 or more levels of progress in English (%)	49	72	Increased by 23
(FFTD = 71%)			
3 or more levels of progress in Maths (%)	45	65	Increased by 20
(FFTD = 59%)			

Source: Statistical data provided by Packwood School.
Note: FFTD Target = the Fischer Family Trust target to place the school in the national top 25 *percentile*.

References

Adams, J., Kahn, R. and Katz, D. (1980), *The Study of Organizations*. San Francisco, CA: Jossey-Bass.

Albritton, R. (1995), 'Perceptions of transformational vs. transactional leadership in university libraries', in R. AmRhein (ed.) *Continuity and Transformation: The Promise of Confluence*. Proceedings of the 7th National Conference of the Association of College and Research Libraries.

Anderson, D. and Anderson, L. (2001), *Beyond Change Management: Advanced Strategies for Today's Transformational Leaders*. San Francisco, CA: Pfeiffer.

Armstrong, M. (2004), *How to Be an Even Better Manager: A Complete A-Z of Proven Techniques and Essential Skills*, 6th Edition. London: Kogan Page.

Auld, R. (1976), *William Tyndale, Junior and Infant Schools Public Inquiry*. A Report to the Inner London Education Authority. London: Inner London Education Authority.

Ball, S. (2006), *Education Policy and Social Class: The Selected Works of Stephen J. Ball*. New York: Routledge.

Bank, J., Kakabadse, A. and Vinnicombe, S. (2004), *Working in Organisations*, 2nd Edition. Hampshire: Gower Publishing Limited.

Bass, B. and Riggio, R. (2006), *Transformational Leadership*, 2nd Edition. New Jersey: Lawrence Erlbaum Associates.

Bass, B. and Steidlmeier, P. (2006), 'Ethics, character, and authentic transformational leadership' (ONLINE - http://www.vanguard.edu/uploadedFiles/Faculty/RHeuser/ETHICS,%20MORAL%20CHARACTER%20AND%20AUTHENTIC%20TRANSFORMATIONAL%20LEADERSHIP.pdf Accessed 27 February 2010).

Bell, L. (2007), 'Theories of leadership – national & international perspectives', Unpublished paper for the Doctor of Education Leadership and Management (EdD) Course: University of Lincoln.

Bell, L. and Bolam, R. (2010), 'Teacher professionalism and continuing professional development: contested concepts and their implications for school leaders', in T. Bush, L. Bell and D. Middlewood (eds) *Principles of Educational Leadership and Management*, 2nd Edition. London: Paul Chapman Sage.

Bell, L. and Stevenson, H. (2006), *Education Policy: Process, Themes and Impact*. London: Routledge.

Bellingham, R. (2003), *Ethical Leadership: Rebuilding Trust in Corporations*, 2nd Edition. Massachusetts: HRD Press Inc.

Bennett, N. (1976), *Teaching Styles and Pupil Progress*. London: Open Books.

Blanchard, K. (2010), *Leading at a Higher Level*, 2nd Edition. New Jersey: Blanchard Management Corporation.

Blandford, S. (2006), *Remodelling Schools Manual: Workforce Reform*. Harlow: Pearson.

Boone, L. and Kurtz, D. (2006), *Contemporary Business*. California: Thomson South-Western.

Bottery, M. (2004), *The Challenges of Educational Leadership*. London: Sage Publications Ltd.

Bowen, L. (1995), 'The wizards of odds: leadership journeys of education deans' (ONLINE - http://www.eric.ed.gov/ERICWebPortal/contentdelivery/servlet/ERICServlet?accno=ED389708 Accessed 25 March 2008).

Brighouse, T. (2004), *A Model of School Leadership in Challenging Urban Environments*. Nottingham: NCSL.

Broadfoot, P., Osborn, M. and McNess, E. (2000), *What Teachers Do: Changing Policy and Practice in Primary Education*. London: Continuum International Publishing Group.

Brown, A. and Dowling, P. (1998), *Doing Research/Reading Research: A Mode of Interrogation for Education*. London: The Falmer Press.

Bush, T. (2003), *Theories of Educational Leadership and Management*, 3rd Edition. London: SAGE Publications.

Bush, T. (2011), *Theories of Educational Leadership and Management*, 4th Edition. London: Sage Publications.

Cameron, K. (2006), 'Leadership values that enable extraordinary success', in E. D. Hess and K. S. Cameron (eds) *Leading with Values: Positivity, Virtue, and High Performance*. Cambridge: Cambridge University Press.

Chartered Institute of Educational Assessors (2009), 'Driving up GCSE results', in the news (ONLINE - http://www.ciea.org.uk/news_and_events/in_the_news/jim_knight_english_and_maths.aspx Accessed 12 April 2009).

Cheng, Y. (2001), 'The changing context of school leadership: implications for paradigm shift', Paper presented at the symposium 'The Changing World of Leadership: Drawing Together Perspectives on Leadership from Australia, Canada, Denmark, Hong Kong, Scotland, England, and USA' of the International Congress for School Effectiveness and School Improvement, 5–9 January, Toronto, Canada.

Clarke, P. (2005), *Improving Schools in Difficulty*. London: Continuum International Publishing Group.

Clarke, S., Glendon, A. I. and McKenna, E. F. (2006), *Human Safety and Risk Management*, 2nd Edition. London: CRC Press.

Cox, C. and Boyson, R. (eds) (1975), *Black Paper 1975: The Fight for Education*. London: Dent.

Cox, C. and Boyson, R. (eds) (1977), *Black Paper 1977*. London: Maurice Temple Smith.

Cox, C. and Dyson, A. (eds) (1969a), *Fight for Education: A Black Paper*. London: Critical Quarterly Society.

Cox, C. and Dyson, A. (eds) (1969b), *Black Paper Two: The Crisis in Education*. London: Critical Quarterly Society.

Cox, C. and Dyson, A. (eds) (1970), *Black Paper Three: Goodbye Mr Short*. London: Critical Quarterly Society.

Cox, J. (1997), 'Identification of the changes in attitude and pedagogical practices needed to enable teachers to use information technology in the school curriculum', in D. Passey and B. Samways (eds) *Information Technology: Supporting Change through Teacher Education*. Berlin: Springer.

Curtis, P. (2008), 'SATS for 14-year-olds are scrapped', *The Guardian* (ONLINE - http://www.guardian.co.uk/education/2008/oct/14/sats-scrapped Accessed 5 September 2009).

Davies, B. (2007), 'Sustainable leadership', in B. Davies (ed.) *Developing Sustainable Leadership*. London: Paul Chapman Publishing.

Davies, B. and Brighouse, T. (2010), 'Passionate leadership', *Management in Education*, 24 (1): 4–6.

Day, C. (2004), 'The passion of successful leadership', *School Leadership and Management*, 24 (4): 425–437.

Day, C. (2007), 'Sustaining success in challenging contexts: leadership in English schools', in C. Day and K. Leithwood (eds) *Successful Principal Leadership in Times of Change: An International Perspective*. Dordrecht: Springer.

Day, C. (2009), 'Building and sustaining successful principalship in England: the importance of trust', *Journal of Educational Administration*, 47 (6): 719–730.

Day, C. and Schmidt, M. (2007), 'Sustaining resilience', in B. Davies (ed.) *Developing Sustainable Leadership*. London: Paul Chapman Publishing.

DCSF (2009), 'National Challenge advisers', *National Challenge* (ONLINE - http://www.dcsf.gov.uk/nationalchallenge/advisers.shtml Accessed 12 June 2010).

Denny, R. (2001), *Communicate to Win*, 2nd Edition. London: Kogan Page.

DFE (2010), *What are Academies?* (ONLINE - http://www.education.gov.uk/popularquestions/schools/typesofschools/a005582/what-are-academies Accessed 9 November 2012).

DfES (2004a), *Every Child Matters: Change for Children* (ONLINE - http://www.dcsf.gov.uk/everychildmatters/_download/?id=2675 Accessed 12 June 2010).

DfES (2004b), *National Standards for Headteachers*. Department for Education and Skills (ONLINE - http://publications.teachernet.gov.uk/eOrderingDownload/NS4HFinalpdf.pdf Accessed 23 September 2009).

DirectGov (2010), 'Types of school', *Directgov Public Services All In One Place* (ONLINE - http://www.direct.gov.uk/en/Parents/Schoolslearninganddevelopment/ChoosingASchool/DG_4016312 Accessed 19 August 2010).

Donovan, J. (1993), *People, Power and Politics: An Introduction to Political Science*, 3rd Edition. Maryland: Rowman and Littlefield.

Dorfman, P. (2004), 'International and cross-cultural leadership research', in B. Punnett and O. Shenkar (eds) *Handbook for International Management Research*, 2nd Edition. Ann Arbor: University of Michigan.

Drago-Severson, E. (2002), 'School leadership in support of teachers' transformational learning: the dramatic differences resources make', Paper presented at the Annual Meeting of the American Educational Research Association, New Orleans LA, 1–5 April (ONLINE - http://www.eric.ed.gov/ERICWebPortal/contentdelivery/servlet/ERICServlet?accno=ED466032 Accessed 25 March 2008).

Drago-Severson, E. and Pinto, K. (2003), 'School Leadership in support of teachers' transformational learning: drawing from the well of human resources', Paper presented at the Annual Meeting of the American Educational Research Association, Chicago IL, 21–25 April (ONLINE - http://www.eric.ed.gov/ERICWebPortal/contentdelivery/servlet/ERICServlet?accno=ED478250 Accessed 24 March 2008).

Drenth, P., Thierry, H. and Wolff, C. (1998), *Handbook of Work and Organizational Psychology*, 2nd Edition, Volume 4. Organizational Psychology. Neverlands: Psychology Press.

Drysdale, L., Goode, H. and Gurr, D. (2009), 'An Australian model of successful school leadership', *Journal of Educational Administration*, 47 (6): 697–708.

Eagly, A., Johannesen-Schmidt, M. and van Engen, M. (2003), 'Transformational, transactional, and laissez-faire leadership styles: a meta-analysis comparing women and men', *Psychological Bulletin*, 129 (4): 569–591.

Earley, P. and Weindling, D. (2004), *Understanding School Leadership*. London: Paul Chapman Publishing.

Evans, L. (2000), *Managing to Motivate: A Guide for School Leaders*. London: Continuum International Publishing Group.

Fairholm, M. and Fairholm, G. (2009), *Understanding Leadership Perspectives: Theoretical and Practical Approaches*. New York: Springer Science and Business Media.

Foster, P. (2006), 'Observational research', in V. Jupp and R. Sapsford (eds) *Data Collection and Analysis*, 2nd Edition. London: SAGE Publications.

Gillham, B. (2005), *Research Interviewing: The Range of Techniques*. Berkshire: Open University Press.

Glatter, R. (2012), 'Persistent preoccupations: the rise and rise of school autonomy and accountability in England', *Educational Management Administration and Leadership*, 40 (5): 559–575.

Gold, A., Evans, J., Earley, P., Halpin, D. and Collarbone, P. (2003), 'Principled principals? values-driven leadership: evidence from ten case studies of "outstanding" school leaders', *Educational Management Administration and Leadership*, 31 (2): 127–138.

Gorard, S. (2011), 'Are academies working?', in H. Gunter (ed.) *The State and Education Policy: The Academies Programme*. London: Continuum Books, pp. 120–132.

Gratton, C. and Jones, I. (2004), *Research Methods for Sport Studies*. London: Routledge.

Gunter, H. (2011), 'Conclusion: public education and academies', in H. Gunter (ed.) *The State and Education Policy: The Academies Programme*. London: Continuum Books, pp. 212–233.

Hargreaves, A. and Fink, D. (2007), 'Energizing leadership for sustainability', in B. Davies, (ed.) *Developing Sustainable Leadership*. London: Paul Chapman Publishing.

Harris, A. (2002), 'Effective leadership in schools facing challenging circumstances', *National College for School Leadership* (ONLINE - http://collection.europarchive.org/tna/20060731065549/http://www.ncsl.org.uk/media-416-80-effective-leadership-in-schools-facing-challenging-circumstances.pdf Accessed 27 August 2010).

Harris, A. (2003), 'Teacher leadership and school improvement', in A. Harris, C. Day, D. Hopkins, M. Hadfield, A. Hargreaves and C. Chapman (eds) *Effective Leadership for School Improvement*. New York: Routledge.

Harris, A. and Chapman, C. (2002), *Effective Leadership in Schools Facing Challenging Circumstances*. Nottingham: NCSL.

Harris, A. and Thompson, P. (2006), 'Leading schools in poor communities: What do we know and how do we know it?' Paper presented at the International Congress of School Effectiveness and Improvement, Fort Lauderdale, 3–6 January (ONLINE - http://www.coe.fau.edu/conferences/papers/Harris%20and%20Thomson.pdf Accessed 11 September 2010).

Hartog, D. (2003), 'Trusting others in organizations: leaders, management and co-workers', in B. Nooteboom and F. Six (eds) *The Trust Process in Organizations: Empirical Studies of the Determinants and the Process of Trust Development*. Cheltenham: Edward Elgar Publishing.

Hermans, C. and Dupont, J. (2002), 'Social construction of moral identity in view of a concrete ethics', in C. Hermans, G. Immink, A. de Jong and J. Van Der Lans (eds) *Social Constructionism and Theology*. Leiden: Brill.

Hiebert, M. and Klatt, B. (2001), *The Encyclopedia of Leadership: A Practical Guide to Popular Leadership Theories and Techniques*. New York: McGraw-Hill.

http://www.education.gov.uk/egi-bin/schools/performance/archieve/group_o8.pl? (accessed 1 April 2012).

Hybels, B. (2002), *Courageous Leadership*. Michigan: Zondervan.

Jacobs, K. (2007), 'Utilizing the William Allan Kritsonis balanced teeter-totter model as a means to cultivate a legacy of transformational leaders in schools: a national focus' *National Forum of Educational Administration and Supervision Journal*, 25 (4): 1–16.

Jacobson, S., Johnson, L., Ylimaki, R. and Giles, C. (2009), 'Sustaining success in an American school: a case for governance change', *Journal of Educational Administration*, 47 (6): 753–764.

Jorgenson, O. (2006), 'Going private? insights for public school leaders considering the move to independent schools', *Clearing House: A Journal of Educational Strategies, Issues and Ideas*, 79 (6): 265–270.

Kay, W., Francis, L. and Watson, K. (2003), *Religion in Education*. Herefordshire: Gracewing Publishing.

Kurke, L. (2004), *The Wisdom of Alexander the Great: Enduring Leadership Lessons from the Man Who Created an Empire*. New York: American Management Association.

Kurland, H., Peretz, H. and Hertz-Lazarowitz, R. (2010), 'Leadership style and organizational learning: the mediate effect of school vision', *Journal of Educational Administration*, 48 (1): 7–30.

Lambert, L. (2009), 'Constructivist leadership', in B. Davies (ed.) *The Essentials of School Leadership*, 2nd Edition. London: Sage Publications Ltd.

Larson, A. (2003), *Demystifying Six Sigma: A Company-Wide Approach to Continuous Improvement*. New York: American Management Association.

Leithwood, K., Anderson, S., Mascall, B. and Strauss, T. (2011), 'School leaders' influence on student learning', in T. Bush, L. Bell and D. Middlewood (eds) *The Principles of Educational Management*. London: Sage, pp. 13–30.

Leithwood, K. and Jantzi, D. (2009), 'Transformational leadership', in B. Davies (ed.) *The Essentials of School Leadership*, 2nd Edition. London: Sage Publications Ltd.

Leithwood, K., Louis, K., Anderson, S. and Wahlstrom, K. (2004), *How Leadership Influences Student Learning: Review of Research*. New York: The Wallace Foundation.

Liebman, H., Maldonado, N., Lacey, C. and Thompson, S. (2005), 'An investigation of leadership in a professional learning community: a case study of a large, suburban, public middle school', Paper presented at the Annual Meeting of the Florida Educational Research Association, Miami FL, November (ONLINE - http://www.eric.ed.gov/ERICWebPortal/contentdelivery/servlet/ERICServlet?accno=ED494982 Accessed 24 March 2008).

Lincoln, Y. and Guba, E. (1985), *Naturalistic Inquiry*. California: Sage Publications.

Lingard, B. and Ozga, J. (2007), 'Globalisation, educational policy and politics', in B. Lingard and J. Ozga (eds) *The RoutledgeFalmer Reader in Education Policy and Politics*. New York: Routledge.

Locke, E. (1999), *The Essence of Leadership: The Four Keys to Leading Successfully*. Maryland: Lexington Books.

MacBeath, J., Cully, R. and Lander, R. (1996), 'Lochgelly North Special School', in P. Hamlyn (ed.) *Success Against the Odds: Effective Schools in Disadvantaged Areas*. London: Routledge.

Maldonado, N., Efinger, J. and Lacey, C. (2003), 'Personal moral development: perceptions of 14 moral leaders' (ONLINE - http://www.eric.ed.gov/ERICWebPortal/contentdelivery/servlet/ERICServlet?accno=ED476828 Accessed 24 March 2008).

Marquis, B. and Huston, C. (2005), *Leadership Roles and Management Functions in Nursing: Theory and Application*, 5th Edition. Maryland: Lippincott Williams & Wilkins.

Mayer, D. and Clemens, J. (1999), *The Classic Touch: Lessons in Leadership from Homer to Hemingway*. Illinois: McGraw-Hill Professional.

McCartney, P. (1969), *The End*. London: Sony/ATV Music Publishing.

Mercer, J., Barker, B. and Bird, R. (2010), *Human Resource Management in Education: Context, Themes and Impact*. London: Routledge.

Mero, N., Rizzo, J. and Tosi, H. (2000), *Managing Organizational Behavior*, 4th Edition. New Jersey: Blackwell Publishing.

Murugan, M. (2004), *Management Principles and Practices*. New Delhi: New Age Publishers.

Noble, M., McLennan, D., Wilkinson, K., Whitworth, A., Barnes, H. and Dibben, C. (2008), 'The English indices of deprivation 2007', *Communities and Local Government* (ONLINE - http://www.communities.gov.uk/documents/communities/pdf/733520.pdf Accessed 20 March 2010).

Northouse, P. (2007), *Leadership Theory and Practice*, 4th Edition. London: Sage Publications Ltd.

Ofsted (2003), http://www.ofsted.gov.uk/sites/default/files/documents/local_authority_reports/nottinghamshire (Accessed 1 February 2013).

Ofsted (2006), 'Inspection reports' (ONLINE - http://www.ofsted.gov.uk/oxcare_providers/list/ Accessed 11 April 2009).

Ofsted (2007), 'Inspection reports' (ONLINE - http://www.ofsted.gov.uk/oxcare_providers/list/ Accessed 11 April 2009).

Ofsted (2008), 'Inspection reports' (ONLINE - http://www.ofsted.gov.uk/oxcare_providers/list/ Accessed 11 April 2009).

Ofsted (2010), http://www.ofsted.gov.uk/provider/files/963159/urn (Accessed 1 February 2013).

Ofsted (2012), http://www.ofsted.gov.uk/provider/files/1937571/urn (Accessed 1 February 2013).

Owens, R. (1970), *Organizational Behavior in Schools*. New York: Prentice-Hall.

Poster, C., Blandford, S. and Welton, J. (1999), *Restructuring: The Key to Effective School Management*. New York: Routledge.

Potter, D., Reynolds, D. and Chapman, C. (2002), 'School improvement for schools facing challenging circumstances: a review of research and practice', *School Leadership and Management*, 22 (3): 243–256.

Rhode, D. (2006), 'Where is the leadership in moral leadership', in D. Rhode (ed.) *Moral Leadership: The Theory and Practice of Power, Judgement and Policy.* San Francisco, CA: Jossey-Bass.

Ribbins, P. and Marland, M. (1994), *Headship Matters: Conversations with Seven Secondary School Headteachers.* London: Longmans.

Riley, K. (1998), *Whose School is it Anyway.* London: Falmer Press.

Shell, R. (2003), *Management of Professionals*, 2nd Edition. New York: Marcel Dekker Inc.

Smith, P. (2007), 'Virtuous friendship as a model for school leadership', Unpublished Ed course paper: University of Sheffield (April 2007).

Southworth, G. (1995), *Looking into Primary Headship: A Research-Based Interpretation.* London: Falmer Press.

Southworth, G. (1998), *Leading Improving Primary Schools: The Work of Headteachers and Deputy Heads.* London: Routledge.

SSAT (2009), 'Specialist Schools and Academies Trust', *The Schools Network* (ONLINE - http://www.specialistschools.org.uk/ Accessed 1 October 2009).

Stevenson, H. (2006), 'Moving towards, into and through principalship: developing a framework for researching the career trajectories of school leaders', *Journal of Educational Administration*, 44 (4): 408–420.

Sun, J. (2009), 'Comparisons between transformational leadership and the Confucian idea of transformation', in A. Wiseman (ed.) *Educational Leadership: Global Contexts and International Comparisons.* Bingley: Emerald Group Publishing Limited.

Tannenbaum, R. and Schmidt, W. (1973), 'How to choose a leadership pattern', *Harvard Business Review*, May–June: 62–180.

Taylor Webb, P., Neumann, M. and Jones, L. (2004), 'Politics, school improvement, and social justice: a triadic model of teacher', *The Educational Forum*, 68: 254–262.

TDA (2009), 'Professional standards' *Training and Development Agency for Schools* (ONLINE - http://www.tda.gov.uk/teachers/professionalstandards. aspx Accessed 23 September 2009).

Teachernet (2006), 'A resource to support the education profession', *Review of Deprivation Factors* (ONLINE - http://www.teachernet.gov.uk/ Accessed 12 April 2009).

Thompson, P. (1995), 'Constructivism, cybernetics, and information processing: implications for technologies of research on learning', in L. Steffe and J. Gale (eds) *Constructivism in Education.* New Jersey: Lawrence Erlbaum Associates Inc.

Thrupp, M. and Willmott, R. (2003), *Educational Management in Managerialist Times: Beyond the Textural Apologists.* Berkshire: Open University Press.

Tomlinson, S. (1998), 'A tale of one school in one city: Hackney Down', in R. Slee and G. Weiner with S. Tomlinson (eds) *School Effectiveness for Whom? Challenges to the School Effectiveness and Improvement Movements.* London: Falmer Press, pp. 157–169.

Vasu, M., Stewart, D. and Garson, G. (1998), *Organizational Behavior and Public Management*, 3rd Edition. New York: CRC Press.

Verona, G. and Young, J. (2001), 'The influence of principal transformational leadership style on high school proficiency test results in New Jersey comprehensive and vocational-technical high schools', Paper presented at the Annual Meeting of the American Educational Research Association, Seattle WA, 10–14 April (ONLINE - http://www.eric.ed.gov/ERICWebPortal/contentdelivery/servlet/ERICServlet?accno=ED454281 Accessed 25 March 2008).

Weinberger, L. (2004), 'An examination of the relationship between emotional intelligence and leadership style', Paper presented at the Academy of Human Resource Development International Conference, Austin TX, 3–7 March (ONLINE - http://www.eric.ed.gov/ERICWebPortal/contentdelivery/servlet/ERICServlet?accno=ED492518 Accessed 24 March 2008).

Whitfield, D. (2000), 'The third way for education: privatisation and marketisation', *Forum for Promoting 3–19 Comprehensive Education*, 42 (2): 82–85.

Wright, N. (2001), 'Leadership, "bastard leadership" and managerialism', *Educational Management Administration and Leadership*, 29 (3): 275–290.

Wright, N. (2003), 'Principled "bastard leadership"?: a rejoinder to Gold, Evans, Earley, Halpin and Collarbone', *Educational Management Administration and Leadership*, 31 (2): 139–144.

Index

Note: Locators with letter *t* denote tables.